EDITED BY
FLORENCE PALPA
AND ALISTAIR SMITH

RETHINKING
VALUE CHAINS

Tackling the Challenges of Global Capitalism

POLICY PRESS SHORTS POLICY & PRACTICE

First published in Great Britain in 2021 by

Policy Press, an imprint of
Bristol University Press
University of Bristol
1–9 Old Park Hill
Bristol
BS2 8BB
UK
t: +44 (0)117 954 5940
e: bup-info@bristol.ac.uk

Details of international sales and distribution partners are available at
policy.bristoluniversitypress.co.uk

British Library Cataloguing in Publication Data
A catalogue record for this book is available from the British Library

ISBN 978-1-4473-5917-3 paperback
ISBN 978-1-4473-6214-2 ePub
ISBN 978-1-4473-5918-0 OA PDF

Cover design: David Worth
Front cover image: Image of building: iStock/AleksandarGeorgiev; image of
man: Banana LInk © James Robinson

Contents

List of figures and tables   v

Notes on contributors   vii

Acknowledgements   xi

Introduction: Rethinking value chains in times of crisis   1
Florence Palpacuer and Alistair Smith

Part I Mounting issues in the governance of global value chains

one   Global production networks: the state, power and politics   17
    Martin Hess

two   Global inequality chains: how global value chains and wealth chains   36
    (re)produce inequalities of wealth
    Liam Campling and Clair Quentin

three   Orchestrating environmental sustainability in a world of global value   56
    chains
    Stefano Ponte

four   Trade policy for fairer and more equitable global value chains   80
    Louise Curran and Jappe Eckhardt

Part II Strengthening the role of people and democracy

five   Civil society action towards judiciary changes in the regulation of   99
    global value chains
    Marilyn Croser

| six | Assessing the economic, social and environmental impacts of global value chains as a tool for change
Christophe Alliot | 114 |

| seven | Worker- and small farmer-led strategies to engage lead firms in responsible sourcing
Alistair Smith | 133 |

| eight | Empowering local communities in their struggle for land and rights
Eloïse Maulet | 152 |

Conclusion: Pondering the future of global value chains   172
Florence Palpacuer and Alistair Smith

Index   182

List of figures and tables

Figures

0.1	World trade volume, 2000–22	3
1.1	ITUC Global Rights Index 2020	29
1.2	Violations of rights trends	30
2.1	Schematic global value chain illustrating transnational and intra-group transactions	39
2.2	The smile curve	42
2.3	Schematic illustration of 'financial upgrading' where a company is acquired by a private equity fund, reproducing but decriminalising its wealth chain participation	45
2.4	The global inequality chain, showing the regressive tax effects of global wealth chains	47
3.1	Interactions of different kinds of power in the coffee global value chain	63
3.2	Interactions of different kinds of power in the biofuels global value chain	73
6.1	Evolution of the value distribution of coffee products consumed at home, 1994–2017	123
6.2	Evolution of income of coffee growers in Peru, Ethiopia and Colombia, and comparison with the poverty and living income thresholds	125
6.3	Distribution of value, costs and margins of plain dark chocolate tablets in 2018 (cocoa harvest 2017/18)	129
8.1	The four-step staircase	159

Tables

1.1	State roles and state–global production network relations	21
1.2	State–global production network relations and coercive regulation	26
3.1	Changes in power, sustainability and global value chain governance in coffee and biofuels	66

3.2	Overview of orchestration options in coffee and biofuel global value chains	69
7.1	Top ten European lead firms at the top of banana chains, 2020	135
7.2	Evolution of civil society's role in influencing the lead firm to change	148

Notes on contributors

Christophe Alliot has 20 years of experience in value chain analysis, social and environmental impact assessment, fair trade and development issues. In 2012, he co-founded the Bureau for the Assessment of Societal Impacts for Citizen information (BASIC). Since then, Christophe has coordinated more than 30 studies on international and national value chains and their impacts. Before that, he worked for several years in fair trade (Max Havelaar France, Fairtrade International, Alliance of Fairtrade Producers continental networks). As a volunteer, he has also been involved in several French non-governmental organisations (NGOs) promoting international solidarity.

Liam Campling is Professor of International Business and Development at Queen Mary University of London (UK) where he works collectively at the Centre on Labour and Global Production. He is co-author of *Capitalism and the Sea: The Maritime Factor in the Making of the Modern World* (Verso, 2021) and *Free Trade Agreements and Global Labour Governance: The European Union's Trade-Labour Linkage in a Value Chain World* (Routledge, 2021), and is an editor of *Journal of Agrarian Change*.

Marilyn Croser is a human rights activist. From 2012–20, she was director of CORE, the UK civil society coalition on corporate accountability. She is a board member of London Mining Network, a network of organisations which works to support communities affected by the activities of mining companies. Prior to her role at CORE, Marilyn worked on migrants' rights issues, and on the campaign for an international treaty to control the arms trade.

Louise Curran is Senior Lecturer in International Business in TBS Business School (France). She received her PhD from Manchester Metropolitan University (UK) in 1995. Her research interests include the interactions between government policy and trade and investment flows, EU trade policy making, especially in relation to sustainability and EU–China trade relations. She has published widely on these issues including in the *Review of International Political Economy*, the *Journal of Business Ethics* and *Business and Politics*.

Jappe Eckhardt is Senior Lecturer in International Political Economy at the University of York (UK). Most of his research to date has focused on the politics of trade and global value chains. Previously, he worked at the University of Bern (Switzerland) and the Simon Fraser University in Vancouver (Canada). He also held visiting positions at the Chinese Academy of Social Sciences and the University of International Business and Economics in Beijing (China). His work has been published in leading journals and he is the author of the book *Business Lobbying and Trade Governance: The Case of EU–China Relations* (2015).

Martin Hess is an economic geographer and Senior Lecturer in the School of Environment, Education and Development at the University of Manchester (UK). He previously worked at the University of Munich (Germany) and held visiting scholarships at the University of Hong Kong (China), National University of Singapore and the International Labour Organization (ILO). Martin's research interests lie in cultural political economies of space, global production networks, labour and development. His work has been published in leading interdisciplinary and geography journals, including *Review of International Political Economy*, *Global Networks*, *World Development*, *Progress in Human Geography*, *Journal of Economic Geography*, *Geoforum* and *Economic Geography*.

Eloïse Maulet is International Organiser and Coordinator of the transnational NGO ReAct. She has long been at the forefront of international campaigns to stop land grabbing and to end social and environmental damage caused by the Socfin Group plantations. From 2010 her work included operational support and capacity building for organisations in local communities impacted by the plantations across Cameroon, Liberia, Sierra Leone and Ivory Coast. She wrote the counter-report *Développement Insoutenable* on the Socfin case in 2019. She studied Environmental Economics in Paris, before co-founding ReAct in 2010.

Florence Palpacuer is Professor in Management Studies at the Management Institute of the University of Montpellier (France). A former consultant with the ILO, she has been studying global value chains and their social implications since the mid-1990s, with a recent focus on transnational resistance. Her work has been published in leading journals such as *Economy and Society*, *World Development*, *Competition and Change*, *Global Networks* and *Human Relations*. In 2015, she co-founded the Responsible Global Value Chain initiative with Alistair Smith of Banana Link.

Stefano Ponte is Professor of International Political Economy at Copenhagen Business School (Denmark). He is interested in transnational economic and environmental governance, with focus on overlaps and tensions between private governance and public regulation. Much of his work analyses governance dynamics and economic and environmental upgrading trajectories in global value chains – especially in Africa and the Global South. He is the author of several books on these topics – including, most recently *Business, Power and Sustainability in Global Value Chains* (Zed Books, 2019) and *Handbook of Global Value Chains* (Edward Elgar, 2019; co-editor with Gary Gereffi and Gale Raj-Reichert).

Clair Quentin is a lawyer and political economist. Their research interests include (i) the structural relation between the tax state and global corporate capital, (ii) jurisprudential and policy issues around tax avoidance, and (iii) value theory in classical political economy. They are currently based at the Policy Institute, King's College London (UK).

Alistair Smith trained as a linguist and co-founded several not-for-profit organisations working on international and local development issues in Eastern England. In 1996 he founded the Norwich-based NGO Banana Link, which works to facilitate a transition to a sustainable banana economy. Since 2001 he has coordinated the international work of the organisation from Southern France, alongside trade union and small farmer organisation partners in Latin America, the Caribbean and Africa. In 2015, he co-founded the Responsible Global Value Chains platform with Florence Palpacuer of the Montpellier University Management School.

Acknowledgements

We are grateful to the Rethinking Value Chains network, the Responsible Global Value Chains initiative, and the School of Business and Management, Queen Mary University of London, for financing open access for this book. We also wish to thank George Aboueldahab for assistance in preparing the book and Liam Campling for his insightful and inspiring support to this collective project.

Introduction: Rethinking value chains in times of crisis

Florence Palpacuer and Alistair Smith

The need to rethink value chains has gained momentum in public debates during the COVID-19 pandemic, highlighting the vulnerability of transnational production systems to unexpected shocks that could suddenly deprive import-based, consumption countries from access to very basic goods (Gereffi, 2020), while raising poverty levels to alarming thresholds in export-based producing countries where vast numbers of unprotected workers were left without work or a basic income (Kabir et al, 2020; Morton, 2020). The unsustainability of global capitalism has likewise come to the fore with the establishment of a link between deforestation and the decline of biodiversity on the one hand, and the vulnerability of our societies to disease pandemics on the other (for instance, see Tollefson, 2020).

Social inequalities, precarious development and ecological destruction have been longstanding issues surrounding the rise of global value chains (GVCs), but their magnitude and acuteness have now reached such a point that rethinking their premises and core dynamics has become unescapable. Such an endeavour should concern not just GVC experts, academics and students but also a broad array of actors involved in and around these chains, including policy makers, corporate managers, labour unions, civil society activists and the diverse stakeholders with whom they interact, from consumers to workers, indigenous people and non-human living beings on this planet.

Our short book contributes to such a collective effort by combining academic and activist perspectives to offer some informed analysis of key GVC issues such as the generation of greater inequalities within and between countries, the rise of state authoritarianism to discipline activists and workers, and the challenges involved in enforcing greater sustainability measures within these chains. The book further highlights the transformative capacity of civil society initiatives through concrete cases and opportunities for collective action. In the rest of this introduction, we offer a brief overview of the features of GVCs and current challenges, before highlighting the core contributions made by the chapters that follow.

In the age of global value chains, to paraphrase the title of the last *World Development Report* (World Bank, 2020), about half of world trade is estimated to be linked to this now widespread form of organisation of productive activities, whereby the sequence of inter-related tasks involved from the design to the production and sale of a wide range of goods and services is scattered across firms and countries. The seminal work of Gary Gereffi and colleagues drew attention to the rise of this new pattern of work and production in the 1990s, stirring the development of a broad literature on the merits, contributions and risks of the changing configurations of value chains and firms in the global economy. Beyond academic spheres, the concept of GVCs gained growing popularity in international organisations where it guided and promoted development policies based on greater trade and economic openness among nations over the following decades, particularly geared towards Southern countries (for an overview, see Gereffi, 2018).

By the time GVCs had fully established themselves as the new 'doxa' for thinking about the world economy, their growth cycle seemed to have come to a halt or, at least, had reached a new phase of maturity. The turning point occurred with the financial crisis of 2008, when GVCs channelled the ensuing economic crisis of the US to their suppliers worldwide, principally Asian-based. The steep decline in world trade experienced at the time did not lead to a recovery – a return to the pre-crisis growth rate. Indeed, as shown in Figure 0.1, global trade ceased to grow faster than the rest of the economy. Another, perhaps more powerful blow was to come in 2020 with the COVID-19 crisis, leading the World Trade Organization to envision a drop in the volume of trade of 9.2 per cent in 2020 (also shown in Figure 0.1), while foreign direct investment is set to contract by 30 per cent to 40 per cent in 2020–21 (UNCTAD, 2020).

Figure 0.1: World trade volume, 2000–22

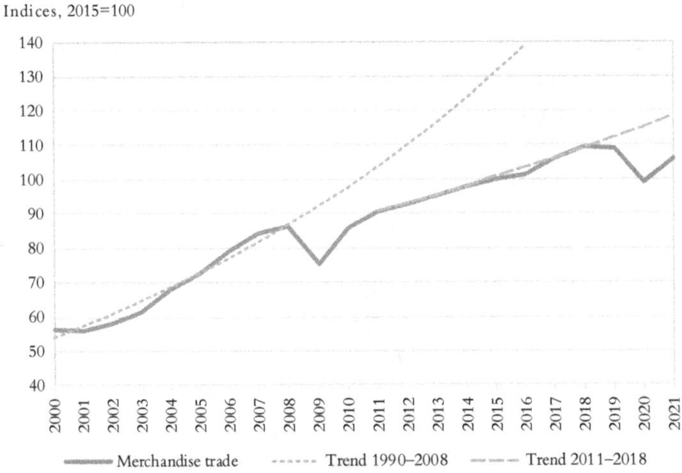

Indices, 2015=100

Note: Figures for 2020 and 2021 are projections
Source: Unpublished data, WTO Secretariat, 2020

If the controversies that surrounded the 2008 crisis were largely focused on the need to regulate financial markets, GVCs found themselves at the forefront of the heated debates stirred by the COVID-19 crisis. The dependencies that decades of de-industrialisation had created in many Northern countries became blatant when the worldwide 'lockdowns' induced a shortage of imported goods that catered to elementary needs, such as medical supplies and drugs. Meanwhile, many workers in Southern factories were abruptly sent home, triggering civil society campaigns to obtain some form of compensation from Northern buyers who had stopped or cancelled orders, as seen for instance in garment GVCs.[1] These shocks shone the spotlight on structural trends that increasingly weakened the capacity of GVCs to act as vehicles for sustainable economic growth and social progress throughout the world. Trends coming to the fore include the rise of inequalities that GVCs were shown to generate among firms and workers, mounting popular discontent among disadvantaged populations, and the ensuing tensions and conflicts among trading blocs and countries (Dür et al, 2020; World Bank, 2020).

The time therefore seems ripe for rethinking value chains, as envisioned in this short book where we take stock of longstanding controversies and mounting critical perspectives on GVCs to highlight and discuss a number of pressing issues and innovative responses that civil society organisations have started to develop.

Indeed, there is a long-running 'battle of ideas' in GVC circles over the merits and limitations of this global form of agro-industrial/industrial organisation. Bair (2005) published an influential assessment of the main transformations undergone by this stream of research initially rooted in world-system theory, highlighting the patterns of power and dependency that global forms of production had created between Northern and Southern economies through the unequal value-capture capacity of the different 'nodes' of the chains hosted by these two groups of countries. From this initial concern with inequalities in the world economy, Bair (2005) recalled, the perspective has evolved towards an increasingly firm-centric, economistic view of 'value chains' – a term borrowed from management sciences – that vaunts the capacity of those firms and countries entering at the bottom, low-value parts of the chains – typically the labour-intensive stages of production – to climb up the ladder via 'industrial upgrading' towards higher value activities that typically involve product development, design and marketing, rather than production or manufacturing.

The following decades saw a burgeoning literature – often but not systematically referring to global 'production networks' rather than 'value chains' – which sought to highlight the political dimensions of these global forms of industrial organisation, their social and institutional context (Coe et al, 2008), as well as the role of ideology and power struggles unfolding among firms, workers, civil society and governments (Levy, 2008), to shape and contest the distribution of value within the chains and their broader societal outcomes (Phillips, 2011; Bair and Werner, 2011).

Environmental critics also emerged, focusing attention on agro-industrial and extractive activities and the unsustainable relationship that GVCs maintained with nature in feeding the world economy (Ciccantell and Smith, 2009). This unsustainability was also shown through a 'financialisation' lens, notably the tight inter-connection that the so-called lead firms – those firms governing the chains and capturing a lion's share of the value created within them – had developed to financial markets, generating a short-termist, profit-driven focus in the governance of the whole chain (Milberg, 2008; Palpacuer, 2008) and a 'supplier squeeze' that results in 'immiserising growth' in producing countries (Kaplinsky et al, 2002; Marslev, 2019).

Over the same period, following the early deployment of GVCs in the 1980s and 1990s, civil society organisations drew on pre-existing transnational connections among labour unions, feminist movements, or development and faith-based organisations to start tackling issues around working conditions in Southern fields and factories, progressively giving rise to a new form of GVC-based activism that targeted lead firms mainly based in the Global North. The aim was to re-establish some form of social responsibility towards workers' conditions in the factories and plantations of the Global South where these firms' goods were being produced.

Over the course of the following decades, GVC-focused campaigns broadened the spectrum of societal issues addressed, from labour conditions to fair trade, low pay, gender inequalities and the environment. These campaigns extended the coverage of GVCs concerned by social and environmental abuses from manufacturing to farming and mining activities. The campaigns also increased the variety of lead firms being targeted, from clothing and sportswear brands to food producers and firms driving other consumer goods sectors such as toys and electronics (Palpacuer, 2019).

In recent years, these two streams of critical approaches have been combined in several hybrid spaces or initiatives involving both academics and activists in sharing knowledge and experiences on GVC-related social/environmental concerns and activism. Among them is the Responsible Global Value Chains (RGVC) initiative launched in 2015 as an internet platform designed to share research, reports and teaching material on social and environmental issues in GVCs, gathering over 90 academics and 30 members of non-governmental organisations (NGOs), labour union federations and think-tanks based mostly, but not exclusively, in Europe, primarily in France and the UK where the initiative was founded. A year later, the Rethinking Value Chains (RVC) collective was formed, with some overlapping membership but with a predominance of activist groups, in order to share information on ongoing campaigns, evolving regulations, upcoming research, and to develop shared projects and campaigns.[2]

This book is an outcome of the encounter of these two networks during a seminar held at the Charles Léopold Mayer Foundation for the Progress of Humankind in Paris in February 2019. It is based on voluntary contributions by several RGVC and RVC members who highlighted key emerging issues in GVCs as well as original civil society initiatives to tackle them. The reflections developed in the following chapters are far from exhaustive in terms of the issues and initiatives being discussed: important topics, such as the specific conditions of women in GVCs, the scope and magnitude of environmental destruction caused by their continuous development, the peculiar challenges faced by fair trade initiatives, and the perspectives and means of action characterising labour unions, do not receive the attention they deserve. There is therefore a need to continue this collective work. Similarly, the civil society strategies explored here do not exhaust the range of perspectives and tools developed over recent decades in GVC-focused activism.

Nonetheless, the challenges being tackled here are among the most pressing and daunting in light of recent trends, including the rise of new forms of state authoritarianism in GVC governance (Chapter 1), the hidden circuits of finance by which the value created by productive activities within chains is extracted and appropriated by capital owners at the expense of states and workers (Chapter 2), and the reabsorption of 'sustainability' into GVC governance as a tool for powerful actors to exert enhanced pressures and extract rents from the chain (Chapter 3). Our collection also includes chapters that address activist perspectives and experiences that have received little attention in the growing literature devoted to transnational campaign networks, such as new opportunities for civil society groups to shape the political agenda of governments on GVCs, particularly via trade regulation in Europe (Chapter 4), the role of activists in the emergence of recent national regulations tackling the social and environmental conditions of GVC-focused activities (Chapter 5), the strategic use of data and quantification to draw public and policy makers' attention to GVC issues (Chapter 6) and the possibilities for bottom-up, South-driven activism to be effectively supported by transnational campaigns (Chapters 7 and 8).

While GVC analysis typically focused on corporations as the architects of the globalisation of production, our critical perspective emphasises the role of the state in shaping and regulating global production, and reassesses its role in the light of recent GVC transformations, along a common thread running through the four chapters contributed by academic writers that form the first part of this book. In the first contribution, Martin Hess reviews the ways in which the state has traditionally been perceived in GVC analysis, highlighting its assignation to a supportive, facilitative role for economic development that overlooked the use of violence and other modes of coercion. Not only have authoritarian forms of state action always been present in GVC regulation, Hess argues, but new forms of 'authoritarian neoliberalism' are actually on the rise, and he calls for much greater attention to be devoted to the exercise of coercion on populations contributing to GVC activities in both Northern and Southern countries.

Liam Campling and Clair Quentin tackle another widely overlooked role of the state in GVCs: its redistributive capacity as a central institution to garner and reinject some of the wealth generated by productive activities into core services for society, such as health and education. Their innovative framework, the global inequality chain, articulates GVCs with global wealth chains (GWCs) formed of financial flows that span networks of tax havens, diverting wealth from public taxation into private forms of accumulation. Hence, in their view, not only are workers deprived of an important part of the value they create through production via the rent-capture capacities of lead firms and other powerful intermediaries in GVCs, but also states are robbed of their redistributive role and capacity to sustain the public needs of societies.

Stefano Ponte has also chosen to emphasise the role of the state as 'orchestrator' of a variety of policy instruments to promote environmental sustainability in GVCs. Ponte takes stock of the limitations of private initiatives that have mainly reabsorbed issues of sustainability into their economic rationale. He reflects on the diverse ways in which sustainability could be tackled by public actors, comparing two GVCs that have highly dissimilar characteristics in terms of power structures, technological constraints and regulatory initiatives. While coffee GVCs, where economic power is highly concentrated at particular nodes, offered little room for manoeuvre for public players, in the case of the more recently formed biofuel GVCs dominant positions were less strongly established and public action had more chance of shaping the environmental sustainability agenda. Ponte emphasises the need to target public action via appropriate instruments – and at appropriate geographical levels – according to the specificities of various GVC configurations.

Louise Curran and Jappe Eckhardt in turn investigate public policy options at the level of the EU, focusing on how trade regulation could promote greater social and environmental protection in GVCs. Their chapter points out some key institutional constraints that need to be worked through when it comes to the proposals that activists could advocate, and explores the options offered by the EU's bilateral free trade agreements and the clauses they include on trade and sustainable development. A first advocacy option pertains to the ratification and application of conventions related to environmental sustainability, such as the Paris Climate Accord, that the EU requires of its trading partners. Parallel pressure would have to be exerted in order to strengthen the effectiveness of monitoring mechanisms attached to such commitments, and to ensure the adoption of dispute settlement systems and sanctions that would be as effective as those laid out in other chapters of the FTAs. Other options discussed relate to the Generalized System of Preferences Plus (GSP+) regime, citing concrete cases of civil society mobilisation that underscore the feasibility and effectiveness of such initiatives.

The second part of the book gives voice to activists who reflect on the initiatives launched by their own civil society organisations in recent years. Marilyn Croser highlights the seminal work of CORE, the corporate responsibility coalition formed by civil society groups in the UK in 1998, in pushing for the adoption of legislation that would require companies to identify and mitigate human rights risks and impacts in their value chains. Her chapter offers an overview of major European legislative initiatives designed either to promote greater corporate supply chain transparency, such as the EU Non-Financial Reporting Directive and the UK Modern Slavery Act, or to establish specific duties and sanctions for human rights abuses resulting from corporate negligence, such as the French Duty of Vigilance law and a similar initiative under consideration in Switzerland. At various stages of designing a regulatory framework, Croser explores the complex stakes of coalition building, the choice of campaigning options, and the ways to counteract business attempts to circumvent new rules that CORE had to work through. She also highlights the levers which could be used in future advocacy work, such as strengthening monitoring processes in existing legal frameworks, and scaling up coalition work at the European level.

Another type of civil society strategy is explored by Christophe Alliot in the chapter devoted to the French initiative BASIC, the Bureau of Societal Analysis for Citizens' Information, established in 2013 with the specific aim of producing objectivised information on the social and environmental costs generated by the GVCs. Alliot lays out the specific challenges faced by BASIC in accessing and modelling the data needed to evidence the highly unequal distribution of value within a variety of GVCs such as cocoa and coffee, on which the small research-oriented activist group has produced several reports. These include the growing paucity of the kind of aggregate data needed to assess the actual economic power and profit margins of powerful players such as lead firms and transnational traders in the GVCs under study; at the other end of the chain, another challenge consists in assessing the resources required for small-scale producers to survive at the beginning of GVCs. BASIC thus tackles the classic 'framing' issue highlighted by social movement theory in original ways, by calculating and demonstrating specific distributional issues and inequalities generated by GVCs governance along the chain.

In the following chapter, Alistair Smith analyses the pivotal role of another small civil society group, the UK-based Banana Link (BL), in structuring strategic actions in the GVCs of one of the most widely consumed food products worldwide – dessert bananas. The initiative launched in 1996 developed an original approach by supporting two traditionally weak stakeholder groups at the production stage of banana GVCs to join forces and build up scale for obtaining a more equitable share of the value created along the chain. The key players are small independent producer organisations located in the Caribbean and South America on the one hand, and independent workers' unions representing men and women employed in the large plantations of eight Latin American countries on the other, all exporting to the European market. BL facilitated the emergence of a 'South–South–North' advocacy network involving a number of other European-based civil society and fair trade groups to support and channel the demands of Southern workers and producers towards the large European buyers. Smith analyses the processes of coalition building that allowed for the activist voices to be amplified while remaining Southern-driven, as well as the specific conditions under which concrete gains could be obtained from retailers in the context of an activist-founded multi-stakeholder initiative, the World Banana Forum (WBF). As a result of the long civil society-led preparatory process, the WBF tackles the sensitive issues of distribution of value along the chain, as well as labour standards, gender equity, labour relations, environmental impacts and how to develop climate-resilient agroecological production systems, under the all-encompassing umbrella of 'sustainable production and trade'.

The last chapter uncovers the main intervention methodology of small France-based civil society network ReAct (Réseaux pour l'Action collective internationale), established in 2010 to support and promote community organising in territories affected by the activities of large French multinationals, notably in African-based agricultural and mining chains. Eloïse Maulet focuses on the case of an ongoing campaign against the Bolloré group and its Socfin subsidiary, owner of rubber and oil palm plantations in nine African countries (and Cambodia) where living conditions are deeply affected by water pollution, deforestation, and the use of violence notably against women, all linked to the multinational's implantation. The chapter unveils the specific steps by which ReAct supported the emergence of organised movements in the affected communities and helped to convey, through transnational network-building, local demands to the corporate headquarters. Acknowledging the difficulties involved in rebalancing highly unequal power relations in GVCs, Maulet highlights the importance of building movements for empowerment and emancipation in the most affected communities.

The significant contributions presented in this set of case studies are analysed in our concluding chapter, where we adopt a Gramscian lens to reflect on the changing forms of hegemony in GVCs, the pivotal role of the state, and the innovative approaches of civil society organisations to maintaining and consolidating a counter-hegemonic front in the contemporary world economy.

Notes

[1] See for instance, the #PayYourWorkers campaign at https://cleanclothes. org/campaigns/covid-19

[2] See www.responsibleglobalvaluechains.org/ and www.bananalink.org.uk/ about/rethinking-value-chains/

References

Bair, J. (2005) Global capitalism and commodity chains: looking back, going forward, *Competition and Change*, 9(2): 153–80.

Bair, J. and Werner, M. (2011) The place of disarticulations: global commodity production in La Laguna, Mexico, *Environment and Planning-Part A*, 43(5): 998–1015.

Ciccantell, P. and Smith, D. (2009) Rethinking global commodity chains: integrating extraction, transport, and manufacturing, *International Journal of Comparative Sociology*, 50(3–4): 361–84.

Coe, N., Dicken, P. and Hess, M. (2008) Global production networks: realizing the potential, *Journal of Economic Geography*, 8: 271–95.

Dür, A., Eckhardt, J. and Poletti, A. (2020) Global value chains, the anti-globalisation backlash, and EU trade policy: a research agenda, *Journal of European Public Policy*, 27(6): 944–56.

Gereffi, G. (2018) *Global Value Chains and Development: Redefining the Contours of 21st Century Capitalism*, Cambridge University Press.

Gereffi, G. (2020) What does the COVID-19 pandemic teach us about global value chains? The case of medical supplies, *Journal of International Business Policy*, 3(3): 287–301.

Kabir, H., Mapple, M. and Husser, K. (2020) The impact of COVID-19 on Bangladeshi readymade garment (RMG) workers, *Journal of Public Health*, 43(1): 47–52, doi: 10.1093/pubmed/fdaa126.

Kaplinsky, R., Morris, M. and Readman, J. (2002) The globalisation of product markets and immiserising growth: lessons from the South African furniture industry, *World Development*, 30(7): 1159–77.

Levy, D.L. (2008) Political contestation in global production networks, *Academy of Management Review*, 33(4): 943–63.

Marslev, K. (2019) The political economy of social upgrading: a class-relational analysis of social and economic trajectories of the garment industries of Cambodia and Vietnam, unpublished PhD thesis, Roskilde University.

Milberg, W. (2008) Shifting sources and uses of profits: sustaining US financialization with global value chains, *Economy and Society*, 37(3): 420–51.

Morton, J. (2020) On the susceptibility and vulnerability of agricultural value chains to COVID-19, *World Development*, 136, doi: 10.1016/j.worlddev.2020.105132.

Palpacuer, F. (2008) Bringing the social context back in: governance and wealth distribution in global commodity chains, *Economy and Society*, 37(3): 393–419.

Palpacuer, F. (2019) Contestation and activism in global value chains, in Gereffi, G., Ponte, S. and Raj-Reichert, G. (eds) *Handbook on Global Value Chains*, Edward Elgar Publishing, pp 199–213.

Phillips, N. (2011) Informality, global production networks and the dynamics of 'adverse incorporation', *Global Networks*, 11(3): 380–97.

Tollefson, J. (2020) Why deforestation and extinctions make pandemics more likely, *Nature*, 584: 175–6.

UNCTAD (2020) Coronavirus could cut global investment by 40%, new estimates show, 26 March, https://unctad.org/news/coronavirus-could-cut-global-investment-40-new-estimates-show

World Bank (2020) *World Development Report 2020: Trading for Development in the Age of Global Value Chains*, World Bank.

World Trade Organization (2020) Trade shows signs of rebound from COVID-19, recovery still uncertain, Press release, 6 October.

PART I

Mounting issues in the governance of global value chains

ONE

Global production networks: the state, power and politics

Martin Hess

Introduction

It has become almost a truism that global value chains (GVCs) and global production networks (GPNs) have become a central feature of the contemporary global economy. Powerful lead firms such as Glencore, Apple (the first US company in the world to be valued at US$2 trillion on Wall Street, and only the second in the world after oil giant Saudi Aramco), Airbus or Zara orchestrate the configurations and geographies of these value chains and networks – from extractive industries to software development, aircraft production to garment manufacturing. As GVCs and GPNs have become ever more prevalent phenomena over the last four decades, their importance has been recognised by global institutions such as the World Bank, the International Monetary Fund (IMF) and the International Labour Organization (ILO) to formulate economic and social policies and initiatives. In the same vein, social sciences have developed sophisticated analytical frameworks and theories to explain their development, governance and impact on the global economy (Coe and Yeung, 2015; Gereffi, 2018).[1] However, recent major events and more gradual global shifts have cast some doubt on the future of GPNs, their organisation and geographies, among the public, policy makers and academics alike.

Since the global expansion of neoliberalism from the 1980s onwards, the world economy faced its first major shock in the form of the global financial crisis of 2007/08. This crisis was followed by a second inflection point when the COVID-19 pandemic hit the world in 2020, temporarily shutting down many national economies first in Asia, then Europe, the Americas and Africa leading to recessions in many countries not seen since the Great Depression of the 20th century. Both crises highlighted not only the problems and perils of neoliberalism but also brought into sharp relief the vulnerabilities of a globally interconnected economic system which had seemingly eschewed oversight and regulation by the state and global institutions. In between these two global crisis moments, there were related yet more incremental political-economic developments which added to creating potential new trends and clearly accelerating existing ones affecting GPNs, for instance widespread austerity policies adopted by many nation states in Europe and beyond adding to growing inequality. Taken together, this arguably led to a new wave of right-wing populism and increasing nationalism in various parts of the world, epitomised by the 2016 referendum decision of the UK to leave the EU (Brexit) and the 2016 election of Donald Trump as President of the United States, both aimed at reasserting a perceived (and reactionary) nation-state sovereignty (under the slogans 'Take Back Control' and 'America First', respectively). To this, the current trade disputes between the US and China can be added as the latest manifestation of political and economic challenges with which firms and other actors in GPNs are confronted.

While the Sino-US trade war and Brexit tend to dominate the headlines in public discourse and academic analysis, and have far-reaching potential and real consequences for the architectures and geographies of GPNs, they are by no means the only signs of a growing trend towards political and forceful state involvement in the global economy. Looking at states like India, Turkey or Brazil, among other examples, a trend to a renewed state involvement in economic governance – which had been assumed to be substantially relegated under global neoliberalism – is emerging that also exhibits increasingly authoritarian forms of politics. The developments outlined may help to illustrate the state as fundamental and integral to the workings of GPNs, not only since the crises and austerity policies of the 21st century, but also in previous periods. As recent literature has demonstrated (Horner, 2017; Horner and Alford, 2019; Werner, 2020), the state as an actor in GPNs has always assumed various important roles and functions; however, there still remains a need to reflect more on the nature of the state, politics and power as increasingly authoritarian, including a new emphasis on coercive governance versus networked forms which were assumed to be largely the norm in the past.

The following discussion builds on and tries to synthesise insights from existing work on state–GPN relations, and to contextualise it in light of the recent political and economic crises and transformations. More specifically, the chapter aims to achieve three goals, namely: a) revisiting the regulatory role of the state and how it penetrates other state roles in value chains and production networks; b) exploring the nature of the state and its relation to GPNs through existing concepts and the lens of Antonio Gramsci's concept of the integral state; and c) highlighting increasing state authoritarianism and related forms of coercive governance, including the mechanisms through which this is achieved. These three points will then be illustrated using examples of labour governance in GPNs, as labour is arguably the most important and also the most politically contested element of global production.

Reconsidering state roles in GPNs

GPNs and GVCs have been broadly defined as organisational arrangements, coordinated by powerful lead firms, and linking suppliers, producers, consumers and states in the world economy. While the role of the state has long been recognised, albeit to varying degrees, the by now extensive conceptual and empirical literature on GVCs nevertheless has usually placed the firms as actors centre stage, with comparatively little attention to the state as a major player and inextricable part of GPNs and value chains. Rather, it is treated as an institutional environment, structural feature or external power that firms in GVCs have to deal with. As Horner (2017: 4) argued, the GPN framework addresses the state as an actor more explicitly:

> To date, and for the most part, the state has not been fully incorporated into the most widely regarded conceptualisations of GVCs and economic development. Greater consideration is warranted of the variety of roles that states can play within GVCs. ... With greater attention to non-firm actors and by seeing the state as an integral part of a network, rather than an external influence, the GPN approach has the potential to address not just how the state influences GPNs but also how participation in GPNs influences the state and its policy choices.

Based on this observation, Horner fleshed out the various roles states play, in the form of facilitator and regulator of GPNs, as well as including the state as producer (in the form of state-owned companies) and buyer (through public procurement). While the recognition of the various state roles in GPNs usefully expands the prevailing focus on the state as facilitator and regulator, I want to argue that state regulatory policies – rather than sitting alongside other roles – permeate them in fundamental ways, and therefore need to be seen as

Table 1.1: State roles and state–global production network relations

State regulation and politics		
State as facilitator	State as producer	State as buyer
Examples: Special Economic Zones; free trade arrangements; foreign investment policies; labour laws	*Examples*: state-owned enterprise regulations; sovereign wealth fund investment	*Examples*: military procurement regulations; compulsory licensing of pharmaceuticals
Private and civil society actors in global production networks		

Source: Adapted from Horner (2017)

an overarching element of the state being part of GPNs (see Table 1.1). The distinction made by Horner between facilitator and regulator is based on the argument that the former entails enabling policies whereas the latter is aimed at preventing or curtailing negative outcomes. Yet, facilitating also requires rules to be followed by both foreign and domestic firms, and labour to be regulated in a way that attracts investment, for instance, which both Horner (2017) and Horner and Alford (2019) acknowledge but do not further elaborate.

In this context, facilitating trade has long been at the forefront of state agency, most prominently through free trade arrangements reducing tariff and non-tariff barriers; in recent years, such trade arrangements have become increasingly unilateral in their configuration, negotiated either between individual nation states or between individual states and economic blocs such as the EU. Trade deals also have become increasingly conditional, including for instance labour rights clauses imposed by one party on the other (World Trade Organization, 2020; see also Curran and Eckhardt, this volume). At the intra-national level, a proliferation of Special Economic Zones, Export Processing Zones and Free Ports as a territorial form of 'regulation for facilitation' has also been observed (UNCTAD, 2019), while the latest *World*

Development Report (World Bank, 2020) – aptly titled 'Trading for Development in the Age of Global Value Chains' – calls for developing economies to 'flexibilise' their labour markets in order to more deeply integrate in GVCs.

State power as a regulator and (geo-)politics are also increasingly visible in state agencies' roles as producer and buyer (see Horner and Alford, 2019). Recent examples illustrating this include current and ongoing struggles over countries' access to personal protective equipment, medicines to treat COVID-19, and future vaccines, with ramifications for GPNs producing these; and telecoms equipment manufacturer Huawei from China being banned from involvement in the future rollout of mobile phone networks in the UK for 'national security' reasons, as there are fears of problematic Chinese state influence on the privately owned company. In other words, while Huawei legally is a private company, geo-politically it is seen as akin to a state-owned enterprise.

There is no doubt that Horner's elaboration on the roles of the state in GPNs provides a first major conceptual step towards a more inclusive and explicit consideration of the state, for the GVC framework in particular. Yet, as with much of the existing literature on GVCs, there remains one largely unresolved issue, that is, how to think about the state in GPNs beyond its obvious and powerful roles as an actor in a 'functional' way. According to Glassman (2011), who has called for more recognition of the importance of geopolitics for the formation of GPNs, what underpins most work on GPNs is a neo-Weberian view of the state as a community holding (or claiming) the territorial monopoly of violence and the state being distinct from capital and markets. In his influential paper, Horner (2017) is not explicitly addressing this theoretical issue, but has made a move in the right direction by including state buyer and producer roles which clearly show a much more intricate state-capital relationship which is networked rather than merely territorial. A look at part state-owned companies such as Germany's car maker Volkswagen or France's utilities provider EDF, as well as the state purchasing formerly state-owned but outsourced and privatised goods and services, may suffice to illustrate this point. In a similar vein, recent work on the state in GPNs has moved towards a strategic-relational approach, as developed by sociologist Bob Jessop, that defines the state as a social formation as opposed to a more instrumental reading of state policy. More specifically, 'a strategic-relational reading of the state requires attention to the configuration of social forces underpinning state support for particular policy directions, and how state hegemonic projects provide the basis for accumulation strategies, of which GPNs form one important component' (Smith, 2015: 299).

A strategic-relational approach represents a further important step forward to stronger recognition of state and governance beyond territorial regulation and state-market dualisms as often assumed in neo-Weberian approaches, but some scholars have argued that the theoretical pendulum has swung too far towards a network governance bias, at the expense of more hierarchical and coercive forms of state governance. As Fawcett (2009, cited in Davies 2013) pointed out when reflecting on prevailing governance theories: 'Metagovernance ... not only indicates a continued role for the state in the regulation of self-regulating governance networks, but it also casts doubt on the view that the vertical hierarchies of the old social structures of the state have been replaced or subsumed by such networks.' In the more specific context of GPNs, the argument that states have shifted from an active role in deregulation policies towards a more authoritarian interventionist role has also been put forward (Meyer and Phillips, 2017).

Most recently, Werner (2021) has provided a more comprehensive overview of the extant literature on the state and global production, including the seminal work of Glassman (2011), Horner (2017) and Smith (2015). In her review, she points towards a range of existing work on the role of the state beyond facilitator, inspired by different concepts including neo-Marxian and neo-Gramscian approaches to highlight the political nature of systems of global production. A useful way to do this as well as to emphasise the intricate connections between state and civil society more specifically lies in applying the Gramscian lens of the integral state, an idea to which I will now turn.

GPNs and the integral state

As I have argued in the previous section, looking at the different roles of the state and its relative power is an important advance in rethinking GVCs and GPNs, but often rests on the idea of a neo-Weberian state that works through its various agencies to facilitate and regulate. While this includes the possibility of coercion it nevertheless has a focus chiefly on one dimension: coercion through administration. According to thinkers such as Friedrich Engels, writing as early as the 19th century, states have both inward and outward facing coercive functions (Davies, 2013) and both are relevant for the formation of GPNs. Again, the US–China trade war provides a convincing example of this, and I will illustrate this further in the next section. Defining the state as a configuration of social forces – as in the strategic-relational approach adopted by Smith (2015) and others – has opened up space for a wider understanding that recognises the power and agency of the state, comprised of social and class relations, and thus aligns more closely with Antonio Gramsci's concept of the 'integral state'. According to Gramsci (1980), the integral state works through both consent and coercion, where the former operates through political society and the latter through civil society, in a dialectical relationship. Building consensus is necessary to afford the state (or political society) legitimacy, whereas coercion is necessary to maintain state hegemony, both inwards and outwards. In this view, therefore, coercion is and always has been present, rather than being the exception. In recent years, however, it seems that state coercion has become increasingly overt and violent, both symbolically and materially.

Along with the rise of GPNs as a predominant form of global economic organisation under neoliberalism, there also has been a concomitant proliferation of corporate social responsibility (CSR) and multi-stakeholder initiatives (MSIs) involving firms and civil society with the aim of effecting positive social and environmental change and mitigating the negative outcomes of GPN operations including poor working conditions and environmental destruction. Indeed, MSIs have become a widespread form of private GPN governance to compensate for what has been identified as a global regulatory gap in which private governance through CSR has increasingly replaced public governance through state regulation (see Arnold and Hess, 2017, for this and the following arguments). However, the GPN and GVC literature examining CSR and MSIs tends to rest on the same assumption of a state-market separation evident in neo-Weberian state concepts. Consequently, it has been argued that centralised state power to govern GPNs has been declining and was replaced by a more diffused private power of corporations and civil society organisations. Using Gramsci's concept of the integral state avoids such dualisms and conceives of state power as both centralised and diffuse, rather than either/or.

In a similar vein, governance scholar Jonathan Davies (2013: 24–6) distinguished five indirect and direct modalities of coercion a state might use and enact. The first, and closest to consensual rather than antagonistic politics and network relations, is *hegemony*, or the enrolment of civil society where citizens (including civil society actors in GPNs) internalise the 'rules of the game'. A second modality is political *threat*, where more consensual and networked forms of governance may fail. Among the direct modalities of coercion, Davies considers *violence* (through the police, military or paramilitary forces for instance), *administrative domination* in the form of 'juridical government', legislation and bureaucracy, and finally *laissez faire*, or according to Gramsci, a ' "deliberate policy, conscious of its own ends ... a political programme ... to change the

Table 1.2: State–global production network relations and coercive regulation

The integral state, regulation and politics through coercion		
Repertoire of state coercion		
Facilitator role	Producer role	Buyer role
Examples: multi-stakeholder initiatives; conditional free trade agreements; taxation; labour suppression	*Examples*: disinvestment; bullying/intimidation; fraud/corruption	*Examples*: contract termination; compulsory purchase orders, fraud/corruption
Private and civil society actors in global production networks		

Source: Adapted from Davies (2013) and Horner (2017)

economic programme of the state itself". The repertoire of state coercion in Gramsci therefore encompasses "violence + economic compulsion + administrative domination"' (Davies, 2013: 26; see also Davies, 2014). Table 1.2 provides a summary and integration of the conceptual discussion in this chapter and includes some general examples of the various state roles and forms of coercion.[2]

Many of the issues discussed so far may at first glance seem unrelated to or not specific of the inner workings of GPNs, and thus not strictly relevant or even appropriate to consider, but a closer look reveals important connections between the horizontal and vertical dimensions of GPNs and should be conceptualised as such. For instance, there have been numerous examples of civil society activism (see Palpacuer 2019 for a neo-Gramscian analysis of activism in GVCs) and actions to achieve the goal of judiciary changes in the regulation of GPNs and of land dispossession for accumulation by GPN actors. The concession of large swathes of land in rural areas to foreign investors by the Cambodian Government led to additional struggles for livelihood among many families in the countryside, with large numbers of (mostly female) workers migrating to urban areas and providing cheap labour for the garment industry (see also the chapters by Maulet and Croser respectively in this volume for more examples of land and rights struggles in GPNs and campaigns for legal change).

To sum up, then, I have argued that it is useful and more fully captures the states' exercise of coercive power in GPNs when seen through the conceptual lens of Gramsci's integral state as political-cum-civil society, and taking into account forms of coercion other than administrative domination. While this conceptual lens does not explain the apparent resurfacing of and increasing (symbolic) violence of state coercion, it nevertheless enables a more nuanced understanding of the ways in which GPN governance and GPN territorialities are shaped in the context of wider political and societal struggles. The following section will illustrate this for the fundamental element of labour in GPNs, using examples from Cambodia and South Korea to illustrate both intra- and international coercive state strategies.

'States of discipline': GPNs, the integral state and labour control

In a world of fragmented GPNs it has become increasingly difficult to attribute responsibility for workers' rights violations to lead firms in GVCs. It would therefore be necessary to rely on state regulation to protect labour in GPNs. Yet states aiming to secure the conditions of capital accumulation and integration into GVCs often are either hesitant or unwilling to develop the necessary legislation and enforcement for labour protection to be effective, especially in times when forms of authoritarian neoliberalism seem to be on the ascent. According to Bruff (2014: 116), authoritarian neoliberalisms 'operate through a preemptive discipline which simultaneously insulates neoliberal policies through a set of administrative, legal and coercive mechanisms and limits the spaces of popular resistance against neoliberalism'.

It is of course not new and does not come as a surprise that there exists a continued trend to discipline workers in GPNs, by both governments and firms, with increasing evidence of state authoritarianism and even violence in response to worker activism. This includes for instance government interventions suppressing wildcat strikes through military and police force, enforcing or limiting the movement of workers across space (internationally and domestically), and tightening unionisation law. Firm strategies to discipline workers, meanwhile, seem to aim at increasing the fragmentation of their workforce through the ramping up of temporary contracts, new forms of 'self-employment' in the emerging gig economy, and 'gamification' as a new governmentality tool; all of these tactics undermine worker solidarity in the workplace, locality and across GPNs globally. Such disciplining strategies are of course fundamental to maintain the accumulation of wealth in GPNs, or what has been labelled 'global wealth chains' (see Campling and Quentin, this volume). As a consequence, a 'race to the bottom' still clearly exists and states are often complicit in its continuation, with many countries in the Global South as well in the Global North facing serious violations of workers' rights (see Figure 1.1). The challenges for labour include new legal strategies of labour control, the intensification of control over organised labour and state violence in what has been labelled a 'post-democracy' world (Doucette and Kang, 2018).

To be clear, there has been progress in some arenas such as health and safety, and working conditions, due not least to public–private governance initiatives, MSIs and labour activism. But enabling rights are still most under threat of erosion by the integral state, despite concessions made in many countries such as the introduction and lifting of the minimum wage. Figure 1.2 shows that in more than 80 per cent of countries the right to strike is increasingly criminalised and suppressed, and the right to collective bargaining severely curtailed. There is also a worryingly high number of countries where workers have been exposed to physical violence, among them the Philippines, Egypt, Colombia and Honduras. But even in formal democracies such as the US and the UK, which the International Trade Union Confederation (ITUC) ranks as either systematically or

Figure 1.1: ITUC Global Rights Index 2020

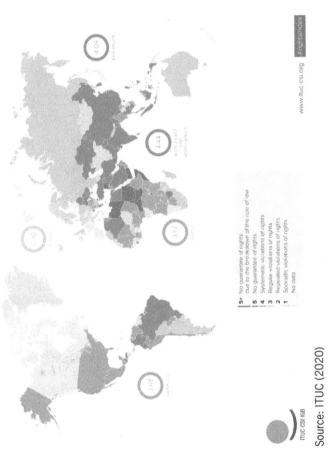

Source: ITUC (2020)

Figure 1.2: Violations of rights trends

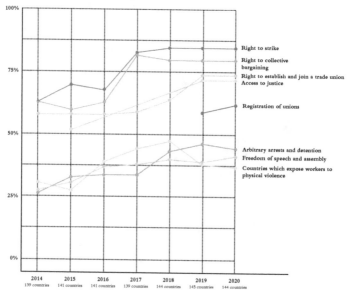

Source: ITUC (2020)

regularly violating workers' rights, disciplining labour through administrative and legal means is rife.

South Korea and Cambodia are just two examples of coercive state-firm-society relations and labour-democracy struggles in advanced and less developed economies. For Cambodia to maintain its position as an important producer within global garment networks, the government has – along with consensus-building strategies such as raising the minimum wage – in recent years also deployed physically violent tactics to supress strikes by mobilising the military to break them up. According to observers, this came about because of pressure by South Korean multinational companies whose factories in Cambodia faced labour unrest, and mediated through the South Korean embassy in Phnom Penh lobbying the military to intervene (see Arnold and Hess, 2017, for a detailed analysis). In the context of South Korea, state coercion relies less on physical violence but nevertheless is present in various forms including legislative means. For instance, South Korean laws introduced to pave the way for labour 'flexibilisation' led to increasing numbers of employees being reclassified by companies including electronics giant Samsung as self-employed. This enabled firms to sue individual workers and trade unions for what they framed as obstruction of business when they tried to assert their rights by going on strike, and thus effectively criminalising engagement in collective action by legally treating it as 'threats of force' (for an in-depth analysis of this case, see Doucette and Kang, 2018). Elsewhere, the ongoing struggles about the employment status of workers in global wealth chains of platform economy transnational companies such as Uber are further evidence of states being complicit in undermining the rights of workers.

Both the cases of Cambodia and South Korea – as well as many more examples of state coercion as described in ITUC's (2020) report and elsewhere – may illustrate the role of the integral state as political society-cum-civil society, the dialectics of consensus and coercion in securing a state hegemonic project, and the various and arguably increasing forms of state coercion that impact on workers in GPNs and beyond. And yet, the potential for labour agency and counter-hegemonic movements exists and collective action by labour and civil society is as important as ever (see also Smith in this volume). Within the literature, this has become the focus of a growing body of work investigating GPNs, labour and development, and the various local, national and international labour regimes that underpin the world of global production (Coe and Hess, 2013; Smith et al, 2018).

Towards deglobalisation and new economic nationalism?

GPNs and value chains still constitute the backbone of the global economy today. Lead firms remain powerful and seemingly untameable drivers to determine their scope, organisation and geographies. The roles of the state in regulating and bargaining with corporate giants as well as other powerful players have long been recognised, but the ways in which nation states as a fundamental part of GPNs are mobilising their power and politics to influence global production has arguably changed. While some of the most powerful states use political pressure to maintain their position among the world's leading economies, other countries use political pressure and coercion to remain favourable locations for global investment and keep being part of GPNs. In both cases, disciplining labour is a crucial component, given its centrality to the production and value generation process in global networks.

This chapter has attempted to rethink the role of the state in a changing world economy made up to a large extent by GPNs. To this end, it has revisited existing and important work on state roles in GPNs, discussed the concept of the integral state as a useful way to theorise the nature of the state and how this might add to current readings of state roles and a strategic–relational approach. Finally, it has emphasised state coercive powers and politics influencing GPNs and the societies they connect, illustrated by looking at these issues through the lens of labour control. In the 21st century, two major global crises as well as more incremental political and economic changes have triggered an ongoing debate in academia and public circles about the future of the global economy and its geography. Following the global financial crisis, there have been voices arguing for a new global economic order characterised by some as 'slowbalisation', while others go further to call for de-globalisation.

Certainly, the spectre of economic nationalism has raised its head in recent years. However, I want to argue that it is too early to conclude that a return to protectionism and the dismantling of GPNs will become the 'new normal' of geopolitics and global economic organisation. The current COVID-19 pandemic has shown that it may have the potential – maybe more so than the 2007/08 financial crisis, Brexit or Trump – to transform GPNs and their geographical reach and configuration. At the same time, however, it also has highlighted that a retreat to nationalist politics – as in the debate about re-shoring pharmaceutical industries for instance – is also fraught with danger, including the possibility of a return to 'beggar-thy-neighbour' politics seen during the Great Depression in the 1920s and 1930s. There is still plenty of work left to further investigate the transformation and future of GPNs, and its economic and societal consequences.

Notes

[1] The concepts of global value chains (GVCs) and global production networks (GPNs) represent cognate yet distinctive analytical frameworks and theories, incorporating the state into their frameworks in different ways. For the purpose of simplicity, the remainder of this chapter uses the term GPN to cover both approaches, unless necessary for clarity.

[2] While neo-Weberian approaches as used in much of the GPN and GVC literature, including on the roles of the state, may arguably not be fully commensurable with the concept of the integral state, Gramsci nevertheless recognises and integrates the different views of a) the state contrasting with civil society, b) the state encompassing civil society, and c) the state being identical with civil society.

References

Arnold, D. and Hess, M. (2017) Governmentalising Gramsci: topologies of power and passive revolution in Cambodia's garment production network, *Environment and Planning*, A 49(10): 2183–202.

Bruff, I. (2014) The rise of authoritarian neoliberalism, *Rethinking Marxism*, 26(1): 113–29.

Coe, N.M. and Hess, M. (2013) Global production networks, labour and development, *Geoforum*, 44: 4–9.

Coe, N.M. and Yeung, H.W.-c. (2015) *Global Production Networks. Theorizing Economic Development in an Interconnected World*, Oxford University Press.

Davies, J. (2013) Whatever happened to coercion? A Gramscian critique of metagovernance theory, paper presented at the Political Studies Association, 27 March.

Davies, J. (2014) Coercive cities: Reflections on the dark side of urban power in the 21st century, *Journal of Urban Affairs*, 36(S2): 590–99.

Doucette, J. and Kang, S. (2018) Legal geographies of labour and postdemocracy: reinforcing non-standard work in South Korea, *Transactions of the Institute of British Geographers*, 43(2): 200–214.

Gereffi, G. (2018) *Global Value Chains and Development. Redefining the Contours of 21st Century Capitalism*, Cambridge University Press.

Glassman, J. (2011) The geo-political economy of global production networks, *Geography Compass*, 5(4): 154–64.

Gramsci, A. (1980) *Selections from the Prison Notebooks*, edited and translated by Quintin Hoare and Geoffrey Nowell Smith, International Publishers.

Horner, R. (2017) Beyond facilitator? State roles in global value chains and global production networks, *Geography Compass*, 11(2): e12307.

Horner, R. and Alford, M. (2019) The roles of the state in global value chains, in S. Ponte, G. Gereffi and G. Raj-Reichert (eds) *Handbook on Global Value Chains*, Edward Elgar Publishing, pp 555–69.

ITUC (International Trade Union Confederation) (2020) *2020 ITUC Global Rights Index. The World's Worst Countries for Workers*, ITUC.

Meyer, F. and Phillips, N. (2017) Outsourcing governance: states and the politics of a 'global value chain world', *New Political Economy*, 22(2): 134–52.

Palpacuer, F. (2019) Contestation and activism in global value chains, in S. Ponte, G. Gereffi and G. Raj-Reichert (eds) *Handbook on Global Value Chains*, Edward Elgar Publishing, pp 199–213.

Smith, A. (2015) The state, institutional frameworks and the dynamics of capital in global production networks, *Progress in Human Geography*, 39(3): 290–315.

Smith, A., Barbu, M. and Campling, L. (2018) Labor regimes, global production networks, and European Union trade policy: labor standards and export production in the Moldovan clothing Industry, *Economic Geography*, 94: 550–74.

UNCTAD (United Nations Conference on Trade and Development) (2019) *World Investment Report 2019. Special Economic Zones*, United Nations Publications.

Werner, M. (2021) Geographies of production II: Thinking through the state, *Progress in Human Geography*, 45(1): 166–77.

World Bank (2020) *World Development Report: Trading for Development in the Age of Global Value Chains*, World Bank.

World Trade Organization (WTO) (2020) Regional trade agreements, www.wto.org/english/tratop_e/region_e/region_e.htm

TWO

Global inequality chains: how global value chains and wealth chains (re)produce inequalities of wealth

Liam Campling and Clair Quentin[1]

Introduction

Inequality within countries and between individuals globally are among today's crucial development issues. These concerns are generally met with a policy response in the form of measures to enhance 'competitiveness' by articulating local firms with the world economy. The principal framing of these measures is by reference to GVCs, which are both the method and units of analysis in a framework seeking to interpret the fragmented muddle of global production (see, for example, World Bank, 2020). Broadly, a GVC is an international chain of market actors bringing commodities from extraction or production of raw materials to the point of consumer retail. The GVC framework has been adopted and adapted by major international financial and development institutions (the OECD, WTO, World Bank, and others), especially for the purposes of framing development aid conditionalities (Neilsen, 2014; Werner et al, 2014).

As it is currently conceived, however, the GVC analytic is a poor lens through which to view wider issues such as wealth distribution and gender inequality, and uncritical deployment of it in a policy making context consequently risks expanding and deepening adverse equality outcomes globally, rather than addressing them. We analyse the key shortcoming of the GVC model as being its uncritical focus on 'value added' at each juncture in the chain. 'Value added' within a market entity means gross revenues minus costs other than wages, or (which is an accounting identity) profit plus wages. By definition, therefore, an uncritical focus on value added as it arises along a chain fails to take into account the distributional effects of the partition of value added into wages for workers and profit for asset owners. It also ignores the further distributional effects of the tax system of the jurisdiction in which the value added arises. This is a serious flaw in the model, since global inequality is increasingly being viewed in terms of the relative tax burdens of the majority of people as compared to large corporations and rich people (Palpacuer, 2008). In addition, an uncritical focus on 'value added' excludes any possibility that value is created elsewhere in the chain, and is merely *captured* rather than substantively 'added' by any firm in which it arises – a process which even mainstream economics is to some extent groping towards with a recognition of the decline in labour's share of wealth (Autor et al, 2017) and the rising market power of multinational corporations and its use to capture higher mark-ups (De Loecker et al, 2020).

This paper addresses these shortcomings by (i) critiquing notions of work and value in mainstream GVC analysis and (ii) expanding the GVC analytic to accommodate the onward journey of 'value added'. Specifically, we expand the GVC framework by integrating it with the related global wealth chain (GWC) framework. The unit of analysis in the GWC framework is chains which 'hide, obscure and relocate wealth to the extent that they break loose from the location of value creation and heighten inequality' (Seabrooke and Wigan, 2014: 257); broadly, they are the routes by which the wealth which arises from 'value creation' accrues to asset owners without attracting significant amounts of tax.

Our framework deploys these two existing analytics as the horizontal and vertical movements of a two-dimensional analytical framework, which we call the 'global inequality chain' (GIC). We use the terms horizontal and vertical to refer to (respectively) the movements of commodities towards consumption and money towards beneficial owners of assets.

The structure of GVCs and value capture

Considering first the horizontal component of the GIC analytic, the global value chain. We are necessarily sketching GVC analysis at the level of its most basic – and widely accepted – insights; for genealogies of and debate on the framework, see Bair (2005), Campling and Selwyn (2018) and Coe and Yeung (2019). Broadly, the GVC places in view a chain – or network – of market actors, one actor's output being another's input until a consumer product is purchased at the end of the chain. The pattern is one whereby (assuming the value chain is read from left to right) processes on the left are raw materials extraction, agriculture and/or standardised manufacture, and towards the right are international logistics and finally retail (Figure 2.1).

Inherent in the idea of the global value chain is that it operates across national borders. As a general rule the processes of production on the left are seen to take place in low- to middle-income countries and consumer retail generally takes place where there is substantial purchasing power. Crucially, there is no presumption that any actor in the chain is under *formal* common control with any other; portions of any given chain may represent the internal processes of a multinational corporate group, while many links in the chain will be between entities which are, on a formal level at least, independent market actors (Figure 2.1).

Figure 2.1: Schematic global value chain illustrating transnational and intra-group transactions

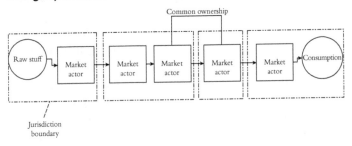

A major strength of the GVC literature is the attention that it gives to the features and mechanisms of coordination and control of firms by other firms intersecting with but not necessarily requiring such formal control: what the literature calls 'chain governance'. The firms exercising control through these governance mechanisms are referred to as lead firms. The principal approach to governance in GVC analysis is a theory of inter-firm linkages as coordination or as 'drivenness' by lead firms over other firms in the chain (Gereffi et al, 2005; Gibbon et al, 2008). Inter-firm relations of control tend to be exercised by lead firms located in nodes of a chain typified by concentration and centralisation and associated high barriers to entry (Hymer, 1979; Nolan et al, 2008). The focus of GVC analysis on exchange relations between firms is insightful because it is an important site of contestation where the *capture* of value can occur and legal arrangements affecting production are set. These can take the form of contracts, private standards and/or other forms of control of production that cut across the boundaries of single firms and are used to capture the surplus value produced within other capitals in the chain and/or to pass on risk and costs.

In GVC analysis 'drivenness' signifies 'a relation of power' (Daviron and Gibbon, 2002: 140), or more accurately *market* power using mechanisms of control – as opposed to necessitating direct ownership – that include quasi-monopoly and/or quasi-monopsony. For example, a lead firm may be able to quasi-monopsonistically capture a share of other players' appropriation of surplus value upstream a chain through the centralisation of ownership of access to markets (such as the relationship of supermarkets to the producers of fresh food); a lead firm may use intellectual property over brands, design and/or technology to pass on costs and risk and capture surplus value from firms competing bitterly to supply components and services in its outsourced global production network (such as Apple, Foxconn and its multiplicity of second- and third-tier suppliers); or a firm may command leadership in a chain through its quasi-monopoly over access to a resource (as in the creation of scarcity in the diamond commodity chain by De Beers). Identifying which enterprises in a GVC actually capture greater portions of surplus value is an empirical question, but the role of capitalist competition in *determining* the form of GVCs and the emergence of lead firms within them is examined, for the purposes of a critique of the concept of 'upgrading' within GVCs.

The policy and mainstream academic discourse is that articulation with value chains is a measure of development success and, outside of local economies, this means procuring from and/or supplying lead firms, whether directly or indirectly (World Bank, 2020). However, this framing misses that these firms 'lead' because they are (at least for a period) the (temporary) winners of capitalist competition in a node (or more) of a GVC. Lead firms incorporate weaker firms and small producers in GVCs and capture value in the sphere of circulation by, for example, limiting the mark-up pricing power of suppliers by encouraging and very often *inducing* high levels of competition among them (Milberg and Winkler, 2013). The implication for workers in such supplier firms is that demands for improved wages or working conditions are more virulently resisted by owners (Baud and Durand, 2012).

Weaker firms and small producers can take many forms. An obvious source of labour-power to them is the countless millions of people who are not paid at levels sufficient for their social reproduction, thereby allowing for the survival of small capitals below the average rate of profit. These include (self-exploiting) petty commodity producers in Africa and Asia, where the work of women and children in the household or extended families is often exploited, unpaid, by men; informalised, casualised and flexibilised workforces the world over; the women who form the majority of China's export-oriented manufacturing workforce, largely rural migrants denied access to social policy in the regions within which they work, and where it is estimated that 80 per cent of even the formal industrial workforce is paid below the legal minimum (Ngai and Chan, 2012); the systematic feminisation of low-paid work (meaning further downward pressure on wages) in firms in Latin America that are articulated with GVCs, reproducing and reproduced by gender relations in local communities; armies of immiserated workers at 'the bottom' of the economy in South Asia; and the millions of people enduring slavery and forced labour across the planet in their adverse incorporation with the world economy.

GVC upgrading and the 'smile curve'

Since the 1970s, economies in the Global South have seen new industries emerge and jobs created, and upgrading is the category used to demonstrate how GVCs offer opportunities for 'development'. In its ideal–typical, linear formulation, upgrading and the capturing of associated 'development' gains involves linking with lead firms in a particular chain (Gereffi, 2001: 1622), and moving 'up' the chain to more rewarding functional positions or to making products that are more profitable and provide better returns to producers (Gibbon and Ponte, 2005; Havice and Campling, 2013). This idea of 'value added' processes which can be used (and in particular can be used, putatively, by market actors in developing countries) to 'add more value' into the chain (and therefore

Figure 2.2: The smile curve

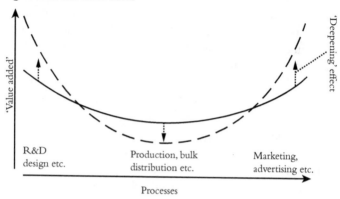

implicitly extract more wealth out of it) is illustrated by the famous 'smile curve' which places actual production at the bottom of a U-bend of value capture, with other processes such as design, branding, marketing and after-sales service situated higher up the horns of the curve to reflect their greater 'value added' (Figure 2.2).

We argue from the perspective of a Marxian theory of value (Quentin and Campling, 2018), however, that the smile curve does *not* reflect actual production of value, and indeed is more or less an inversion of where value is actually produced. Instead, the smile curve reflects the special role that material processes of production play in creating the surplus value which is available for capture. The less well remunerated productive workers are, the greater the surplus available for capture in the system as a whole. But given that surplus value can be captured without ownership of productive assets, the downward pressure on the incomes of productive workers can be exerted indirectly by virtue of the downward pressure on the incomes of firms owning productive assets (such as the diversity of 'small capitals').

The paradigmatic form that such downward pressure takes may be ownership of intellectual property, such as a brand which 'serves as an entry barrier and as a source of unequal distribution of value added in the GVC' (Mayer and Milberg, 2013: 7). But all commercial efforts potentially exert this downward pressure to the extent that they are disaggregated on the level of ownership from material production and distribution. The immediate promise of upgrading, whether real or illusory, is therefore to do the dirty work of exploiting productive labour without being forced to relinquish maximal amounts of the resulting surplus to others. In the longer term, it is to leave behind altogether the risks attendant upon trying to make a profit at one of the core fault lines of capitalism: the one that subsists between productive workers and the owners of means of production. Mainstream discourse regarding smile curves suggests that they are 'deepening', meaning that the 'value added' by processes other than material production is *increasing* as a proportion of total value added (Figure 2.2; OECD, 2013).

Global wealth chains

GWCs are the routes by which surplus accrues to the beneficial owners of capital while attracting as little tax as possible. They include tax evasion and tax avoidance as traditionally understood, the methods used by multinational companies and host jurisdictions to maximise after-tax corporate profits, and tax-enhanced investment strategies such as private equity. They also include onshore subsidies for asset owners such as tax relief on private pensions, corporate tax incentives (see for example the UK's 'patent box' legislation at Part 8A Corporation Tax Act 2010), and other forms of state complicity in tax-free accumulation.

Common themes in GWC analysis are (i) cross-border financial flows, (ii) the use of secrecy jurisdictions and/or offshore banking, (iii) the use of the legal regime of one jurisdiction to undermine another, (iv) the use of intangible assets (which are highly mobile) to shift profits away from the jurisdictions where they are deployed so as to yield profits, and

(iv) financialisation. It therefore brings within its purview such diverse phenomena as money laundering, double tax treaty networks, tax competition between jurisdictions, complex derivative financial products, and collective investment schemes. As with GVCs, scholars who study GWCs are particularly concerned with questions of how the elements of the chain are brought into connection with each other, and how governance is articulated and distributed through the chain (Seabrooke and Wigan, 2014).

Capital always seeks to maximise its after-tax return, and GWCs are therefore potentially positioned as a pervasive phenomenon along the *entire* value chain, rather than being restricted to particular categories of actor. Typically, for example, popular tax justice arguments in the Global North will be levelled at multinational companies, but the owners of a successful small business in a low-income country are just as likely to be evading tax as multinational companies are to be avoiding it (International Monetary Fund, 2015: Appendix VI). Indeed, a corollary to upgrading in GVCs is what might be termed 'financial upgrading' in GWCs, where enhanced participation in GVCs might lead to criminal tax evasion being 'upgraded' to non-criminal tax avoidance. An example might be a situation where a successful locally-owned enterprise whose undeclared profits are being *unlawfully* transferred to an offshore bank is bought by a private equity partnership, with the consequence that its untaxed profits are being *lawfully* transferred to an offshore bank by means of deductible interest payments (Figure 2.3).

GWC analysis deals with the specificities of how wealth is appropriated tax-free at identifiable junctures in the chain, but for the present purposes (which are to do with the overall structure of what we call the global inequality chain) it is only necessary to note five general points. First, multiple entities along the value chain may feed the same wealth chain, as would be the case, for example, where they are all subsidiaries of a single multinational corporate group, whereas other entities in the chain may have GWCs all of their own. The value chain may therefore be

Figure 2.3: Schematic illustration of 'financial upgrading' where a company is acquired by a private equity fund, reproducing but decriminalising its wealth chain participation

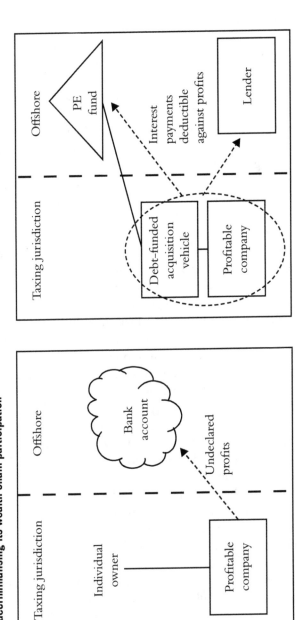

divided into discrete cells of ownership or control and wealth chains are treated as arising from each cell (Figure 2.4). Second, it should be noted that the wealth chains arising from any such cell are likely to ramify towards different specific ultimate asset owners, and indeed where a business is both debt-financed and equity-financed by different persons there will be an immediate bifurcation into two wealth chains. Our schematic deployment of the GWC concept ignores these dendritic wealth chain morphologies for the purposes of simplicity.

Third, the relation between profitability and the percolation of profits up the GWC should *not* be assumed to take place in a chronological sequence of profit followed by percolation; owing to such pervasive GWC phenomena as financialisation and even just accruals-based accounting, it is possible and indeed common for wealth to accrue before cash profits have arisen.

Fourth, where a member of a multinational group is in a tax haven jurisdiction it should generally be treated analytically as part of the wealth chain rather than the value chain. It could be argued that some tax haven entities 'add value' insofar as substantive (albeit materially unproductive) economic activity takes place within them. In these cases the presumption should nonetheless be that the separation of functions which gives rise to that formally distinct business process is driven by the needs of the wealth chain rather than the needs of the value chain. So, for example, in the case of Amazon's UK/Luxembourg tax structuring, the Luxembourg entity had (on a formal level at least) substantive economic functions distinct from the functions being performed in the UK entity. In reality, however, the business operations were conducted without regard to which entity was formally conducting them and the purported separation of functions was found, in a judgment of the High Court, to be 'wholly unreal and divorced from the commercial reality of the situation' (*Cosmetic Warriors Ltd & Anor* v *amazon.co.uk Ltd & Anor* [2014] EWHC 181 [Ch]).

Finally, and perhaps most importantly, in order to analyse the entanglements of GVCs and GWCs it is necessary to

Figure 2.4: The global inequality chain, showing the regressive tax effects of global wealth chains

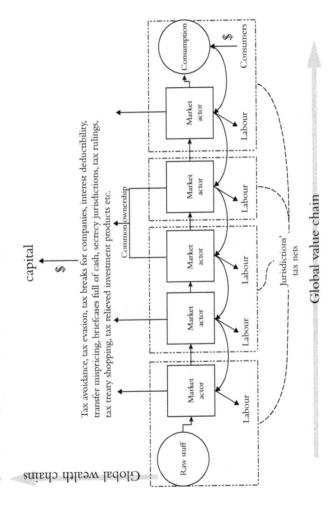

Tax avoidance, tax evasion, tax breaks for companies, interest deductibility, transfer mispricing, briefcases full of cash, secrecy jurisdictions, tax rulings, tax treaty shopping, tax relieved investment products etc.

take a position on the role of intangible assets vis-à-vis the production of value. Broadly speaking there are two positions which may be taken on this (see Quentin, 2020). If one were to adopt what might be classed as a 'subjective' approach to value, for instance in accordance with either the marginalist school or the 'value-form' school of Marxian value theory, one would be likely to treat business functions which give rise to intangible assets as value-producing, in which case those business functions are best characterised as GVC nodes. By contrast if one were to adopt what might be classed as an 'objective' approach to value, for instance in accordance with traditional Marxian value theory or certain neo-Ricardian approaches, one would be likely to treat business functions which give rise to intangible assets as serving to originate instruments of value *capture*, in which case those functions are best characterised as GWC elements.

The reason it is necessary to adopt a position on this question is because intangible assets are de facto GWC elements, insofar as they are deeply and pervasively implicated in specifically tax-enhanced profitability (Collier and Andrus, 2017: 345–7). Broadly speaking it is a matter of moving to tax havens the formal legal assets associated with intangibles and having tax-deductible payments made from other jurisdictions in respect of the use of those assets. In the light of the analysis set out with regard to value creation and value capture as manifest in the 'smile curve', this chapter adopts the approach that business functions which give rise to intangible assets are non-value-producing in any event. This position has the additional advantage that those functions can be treated exclusively as GWC elements rather than complicating composite elements.

At first blush it seems counter-intuitive to insist that no value is being created by the highly profitable businesses in the digital economy, but it is necessary to recall that the vast majority of today's apparently dematerialised business processes are always connected to physical delivery of goods and services in one way or another (Baglioni and Campling,

2017). Uber, for example, may be analysed as a GWC entity attaching to the automotive and petroleum GVCs. Google and Facebook are GWC entities in the GVCs of more or less anything that is advertised. Apparent overlap between wealth chains and value chains nonetheless occurs but it is limited to sectors where the value chain's apparent end product, being not really a commodity but a quasi-commodity arising from legal regimes rather than production, is inherently outside the classical production boundary, such as consumer-facing financial services, residential rental or streaming media.

The global inequality chain

We are now in a position to combine the GVC analytic with the GWC analytic so as to yield the 'global inequality chain': the two-dimensional analytical model proposed in our introduction. The starting point is the horizontal progression of the GVC from raw materials to the point of consumption, with 'value added' arising at each node along the chain. Rising vertically, not from each node of the chain but from each group of nodes insofar as they are under common ownership or control, are GWCs which represent, as an upward path, the journey of 'value added' from business processes along the chain to asset owners. Value is therefore (1) created along the chain roughly in proportion to where the materially productive labour takes place, (2) captured elsewhere in the chain in the form of the 'value added' realised by materially unproductive business processes, and (3) distributed away from the node where it is so captured, as between capital, labour and the state, by reference to the impact of the wealth chains arising from the node or nodes in question.

Each jurisdiction is compelled by GWCs to shift its tax base disproportionately towards labour (and, which amounts to much the same thing, towards consumption of wage goods by workers resident in the jurisdiction) and away from capital. Since labour captures a suppressed share of value from each market actor in the value chain and consumption taxes are proportionally higher for those without a surplus of income to save, the consequence of this is a systemic tendency towards regressive taxation and underfunded states (Figure 2.4).

It is sometimes supposed that imposing the burden of tax on local labour rather than globally mobile capital is beneficial because of the possibility of attracting international investment but in practice the development outcomes have been adverse. This was a hypothesis laid out by Hymer (1970) on the efficiency contradictions of direct foreign investment, which has been variously elaborated since (for example, Ietto-Gillies, 2007), and more recently substantiated by Yamin and Sinkovics (2009) in a review of the literature on tax systems designed to attract investment in low-income countries which found subsequent *declines* in infrastructure investment. But the phenomenon is not limited to the development context: regressive taxation and the underfunding of states is a pervasive phenomenon along GVCs (Lahey, 2015; OECD, 2016), and this is the reason that, when we integrate GWCs into the global value chain analytic, we label the resulting two-dimensional analytic the global inequality chain.

The global inequality chain reproduces inequality, and as an analytical model helps anatomise the ways in which inequality is reproduced, in a number of ways. First, as explained earlier, the general inequalities arising from regressive taxation intersect with specific systemic inequalities along the GVC; for example, the disproportionate burden placed on women in the sphere of social reproduction in circumstances of fiscal constraint.

Second, the global inequality chain analytic makes a contribution to existing critiques of 'upgrading' within GVCs, by foregrounding the risk of increased appropriation of surplus by a market actor in a developing country being ineffective to improve outcomes because it brings with it tax-abusive 'financial upgrading' as described. This might happen in any number of ways. We give the example of acquisition by a private equity partnership, but equally a locally owned firm once acquired by a transnational lead firm will find itself able to take advantage of that lead firm's global tax structuring (ActionAid, 2012).

Third, substantive inequalities in the wealth chain itself are likewise aggravated or reinforced by the tax system, such that wealth flowing from those disadvantaged at value chain level flows to those advantaged at wealth chain level. So, for example the tax system in a specific jurisdiction, in taxing consumption and subsidising private equity, might be seen to effect a transfer of wealth from the customer base of a pharmaceuticals retailer consisting predominantly of low- to middle-income women to the predominantly male high-income personnel of the private equity fund which owns it (Women for Tax Justice, 2014).

Conclusions and ways forward

We have combined analytic frameworks relating to globalised production and consumption and the global tax system to argue that – in their present form – both systems reproduce global inequalities between firms, countries, classes and genders. We argued that the smile curve and related incarnations of a hierarchy of 'value added' in the social and international division of labour are not based on the production of value but its *capture*, principally through legal arrangements of property relations (for example, class monopoly rent). We then linked the GVC with the GWC model so as to map how the burden of tax is predominantly borne by labour rather than capital along the chain. This two-dimensional analytic (i) highlights the class and gender dynamics of value production and appropriation, and the mechanisms by which adverse features of those dynamics are exacerbated and perpetuated through the tax system, and (ii) provides a schematic map upon which specific problems of that nature can be projected.

For those more familiar with the global production system than tax, the key message of our combined analytic is that simplistic 'upgrading' objectives which ignore capital's drive to maximise post-tax profit are of little use in redressing the balance of global inequality. Instead, reallocating the tax burden vertically up the wealth chain towards capital is a fundamental requirement if pursuing such objectives is going to materially (in both senses) enrich anyone other than local elites. For those more familiar with the tax system the key message is that profitability within multinational enterprises may reflect surplus extraction rather than wealth creation; value capture rather than value creation. This means that tax reforms intended to ameliorate global inequalities must recognise the possibility that the tax base constituted by corporate profitability may have to be reallocated for tax purposes not merely to jurisdictions where other group members are active (for example, apportioning tax from a retailer's business activities to the country where products are sold rather than offshore), but outside the corporate group altogether, to elsewhere in the value chain where the value captured by 'lead firms' is actually created (Quentin, 2017). By way of illustration: pursuant to such reforms, taxing rights over the profits of clothing retailers in wealthy countries would largely find themselves reallocated to places like Bangladesh, Cambodia and Indonesia, where the clothing is made and places like China and India where cotton is grown, notwithstanding that the lead firms profiting from global apparel value chains generally have no corporate tax footprint at all in those jurisdictions.

Finally, the combination of the two analytics enables us to theorise certain key features of 21st century global capitalism (in particular financialisation, and the deployment of intellectual property as an instrument of market domination) as operating on two orthogonal axes of contention; the increasing dominance of rent-seeking over production within the private sector, and the increasing dominance of private sector surplus absorption over public sector surplus absorption.

Note

[1] Authorship is equal. This chapter draws on D. Quentin and L. Campling (2018) Global inequality chains: integrating mechanisms of value

distribution into analyses of global production, *Global Networks*, 18(1): 33–56. All figures in this chapter are taken from that article.

References

ActionAid (2012) *Calling time: why SABMiller should stop dodging taxes in Africa*, ActionAid.

Autor, D., Dorn, D., Katz, L.F., Patterson, C. and Van Reenen, J. (2017) *The Fall of the Labor Share and the Rise of Superstar Firms*, NBER Working Paper No. 23396, National Bureau of Economic Research

Baglioni, E. and Campling, L. (2017) Natural resource industries as global value chains: frontiers, fetishism, labour and the state, *Environment and Planning A*, 49(11): 2437–56.

Bair, J. (2005) Global capitalism and commodity chains: looking back, going forward, *Competition and Change*, 9(2): 153–80.

Baud, C. and Durand, C. (2012) Financialization, globalization and the making of profits by leading retailers, *Socio-economic Review*, 10(X): 241–66.

Campling, L. and Selwyn, B. (2018) Value chains and the world economy: genealogies and reformulations, in A. Nölke and C. May (eds) *Handbook of the International Political Economy of the Corporation*, Edward Elgar Publishing.

Coe, N.M. and Yeung, H.W-c. (2019) Global production networks: mapping recent conceptual developments, *Journal of Economic Geography*, 19(4): 775–801.

Collier, R. and Andrus, J. (2017) *Transfer Pricing and the Arm's Length Principle After BEPS*, Oxford University Press.

Daviron, B. and Gibbon, P. (2002) Global commodity chains and African export agriculture, *Journal of Agrarian Change*, 2(2): 137–61.

De Loecker, J., Eeckhout, J. and Unger, G. (2020) The rise of market power and the macroeconomic implications, *The Quarterly Journal of Economics*, 135(2): 561–644.

Gereffi, G. (2001) Shifting governance structures in global commodity chains, with special reference to the internet, *American Behavioral Scientist*, 44(10): 1616–37.

Gereffi, G., Humphrey J. and Sturgeon, T. (2005) The governance of global value chains, *Review of International Political Economy*, 12(1): 78–104.

Gibbon, P. and Ponte, S. (2005) *Trading Down: Africa, Value Chains, and the Global Economy*, Temple University Press.

Gibbon, P., Bair, J., and Ponte, S. (2008) Governing global value chains: an introduction, *Economy and Society*, 37(3): 315–38.

Havice, E., and Campling, L. (2013) Articulating upgrading: island development states and canned tuna production, *Environment and Planning A*, 45(11): 2610–27.

Hymer, S. (1970) The efficiency (contradictions) of multinational corporations, *The American Economic Review*, 60(2): 441–8.

Hymer, S. (1979) The United States multinational corporations and Japanese competition in the Pacific, in R. Cohen, N. Felton, M. Nkosi and J. van Liere (eds) *The Multinational Corporation: A Radical Approach, Papers by Stephen Herbert Hymer*, Cambridge University Press, pp 140–64.

Ietto-Gillies, G. (2007) Theories of international production: a critical perspective, *Critical Perspectives on International Business*, 3(3): 196–210.

International Monetary Fund (2015) *Current Challenges in Revenue Mobilization: Improving Tax Compliance*, April.

Lahey, K. (2015) Women and taxation: from taxing for growth and tax competition to taxing for sex equality, *Tax Justice Focus*, 10(1): 8–10.

Mayer, F. and Milberg, W. (2013) Aid for trade in a world of global value chains: chain power, the distribution of rents, and implications for the form of aid, *Capturing the Gains*, working paper 34.

Milberg, W. and Winkler, D. (2013) *Outsourcing Economics: Global Value Chains in Capitalist Development*, Cambridge University Press.

Neilson, J. (2014) Value chains, neoliberalism and development practice: the Indonesian experience, *Review of International Political Economy*, 21(1): 38–69.

Ngai, P. and Chan, J. (2012) Global capital, the state, and Chinese workers: the Foxconn experience, *Modern China*, 38(4): 383–410.

Nolan, P., Zhang, J. and Liu, C. (2008) The global business revolution, the cascade effect, and the challenge for firms from developing countries, *Cambridge Journal of Economics*, 32(1): 29–47.

OECD (2013) *Interconnected Economies: Benefiting from Global Value Chains*, OECD, www.oecd.org/sti/ind/interconnected-economies-GVCs-synthesis.pdf

OECD (2016) *Tax Policy Reforms in the OECD*, OECD, http://dx.doi.org/10.1787/9789264260399-en

Palpacuer, F. (2008) Bringing the social context back in: governance and wealth distribution in global commodity chains, *Economy and Society*, 37(3): 393–419.

Quentin, D. (2017) Corporate tax reform and 'value creation': towards unfettered diagonal reallocation across the global inequality chain, *Accounting, Economics, and Law: A Convivium*, 7(1): 1–21.

Quentin, C. (2020) A materialist political economy of international corporate tax reform, unpublished PhD thesis, School of Business and Management and Centre for Commercial Law Studies, Queen Mary University of London.

Quentin, C. and Campling, L. (2018) Global inequality chains: integrating mechanisms of value distribution into analyses of global production, *Global Networks*, 18(1): 33–56.

Seabrooke, L. and Wigan, D. (2014) Global wealth chains in the international political economy, *Review of International Political Economy*, 21(1): 257–63.

Werner, M., Bair, J. and Fernández, V. (2014) Linking up to development? Global value chains and the making of a post-Washington consensus, *Development and Change*, 45(6): 1219–47.

Women for Tax Justice (2014) Tampons and tax avoidance, 22 July, https://womenfortaxjustice.wordpress.com/2014/07/22/tamponsandtaxavoidance/

World Bank (2020) *World Development Report 2020: Trading for Development in the Age of Global Value Chains*, World Bank.

Yamin, M. and Sinkovics, R.R. (2009) Infrastructure or foreign direct investment? An examination of the implications of MNE strategy for economic development, *Journal of World Business*, 44(2): 144–57.

THREE

Orchestrating environmental sustainability in a world of global value chains

Stefano Ponte

Introduction

Sustainability considerations are becoming mainstream in corporate strategy and are affecting the functioning of global value chains (GVCs). Production is moving to locations that can meet basic sustainability specifications in large volumes and at low cost. Multi-stakeholder initiatives (MSIs) on sustainability have come to play a key role in GVCs.

Because of this new reality, public authorities cannot shape sustainability only through regulation and international agreement formation. They need to orchestrate sustainability through various direct and indirect, hard and soft instruments, and in ways that take into consideration the power dynamics that characterise different GVCs. In this chapter, I examine the different kinds of power dynamics that characterise two specific value chains (coffee and biofuels), and the role that sustainability issues play in them, with particular focus on environmental aspects. What leverage points can be used by public orchestrators and with what instruments in different GVCs? How can various actions (applying different kinds of power) be used to undermine unequal bargaining positions?

Orchestration for sustainability

The concept of 'orchestration' can help with understanding the role of public actors can play in shaping sustainability in a GVC context – as the conductor of an orchestra seeks to make musicians work towards a common goal, public authorities seek to combine different kinds of instruments for the public good (Abbott and Snidal, 2009). Usually, two broad sets of orchestrating mechanisms are operated: 'directive' and 'facilitative'. On the one hand, directive orchestration relies on the authority of the state and seeks to incorporate private initiatives into its regulatory framework (through mandating principles, transparency, codes of conduct). On the other hand, facilitative orchestration relies on softer instruments, such as the provision of material and ideational assistance (financial and technical support, endorsement) and is used to kick-start new initiatives and/or to further shape and support them. Successful public governors often use a *combination* of mechanisms in attempting to achieve policy goals. But outcome effectiveness is linked to different overlaps of these mechanisms that are GVC-specific, rather than to the superiority of one governance form or institutional setting over another. In other words, we can expect more successful orchestration when public authorities employ a combination of substantial directive and facilitative instruments.

Lister et al (2015) propose two other factors that can enable public orchestration in successfully addressing sustainability issues along GVCs: *issue visibility* and *interest alignment*. On *issue visibility*, we can expect more potential for orchestration if the product, industry and/or related set of environmental issues are visible to the general public, and particularly to consumers. This can occur because the environmental issue itself is obviously visible (such as accumulating trash on urban streets, or dark exhaust fumes coming from ships) or because it is rendered so through consumer labels, public campaigns or social media exposure. Therefore, orchestration is more likely to succeed in GVCs that handle consumer-facing and branded products and/or in those that have been targeted by social movements and the media. When an environmental issue is not clearly visible to key stakeholders, orchestration efforts should include instruments that can enhance visibility.

On *interest alignment*, we can expect better orchestration possibilities if there is substantial overlap between public and private interests (Schleifer, 2013). Because different value chain nodes are regulated by different authorities, there may be different kinds of (mis)alignments between private and public sector interests in different GVC nodes. While it is rare for interests to be aligned at all nodes, alignment at key nodes can provide a strong entry point for orchestrators to stimulate the transmission of environmental improvements along the whole GVC. An additional complication is that alignment between public and private sector interests may differ in different group of countries (such as coffee producing countries in the Global South and coffee consuming countries in the Global North). In any case, interest alignment is not static and should be addressed as a specific objective of orchestration.

Governance and power in GVCs

The term GVC refers to the full range of activities that firms, farmers and workers carry out to bring a product or service from its conception to its end use, recycling or reuse. These activities can include design, production, processing, assembly, distribution, maintenance, disposal/recycling/reuse, marketing, finance and consumer services. In this context, 'lead firms' are groups of firms that operate at particular functional positions along the chain and that are able to shape who does what along the chain, at what price, using what standards, to which specifications, and delivering in what form and at what point in time (Gereffi et al, 2005). GVCs can be unipolar, bipolar or multipolar – depending on how many groups of lead firms play a dominant role in shaping it and on whether civil society organisations, social movements, consumer groups, networks of experts and policy makers, and MSIs for sustainability also play a role in governing them.

Various levels of state action and authority have important structuring effects on GVCs (Horner, 2017). States can act as intentional orchestrators of GVCs, regulate (or deregulate) their functioning, and choose to redistribute (or not) the extra wealth generated through GVCs. States can also be important direct actors in GVCs, for example through state-owned enterprises and public procurement. This is why the concept of public orchestration comes handy in combination with analyses of governance and power in GVCs.

To further understand governance dynamics, we should also examine the power dynamics that underpin them. Dallas et al (2019) propose two dimensions of power in GVCs: a *transmission mechanism* and an *arena of actors*. The *transmission mechanism* of power is anchored by two ideal types: direct and diffuse. On the one end are circumstances where GVC actors (individually or collectively) seek to exert direct forms of influence over other actors or actor groups. On the other end are more diffuse forms of power where the actors or collectives and the objects of power may be less clearly identifiable, and actions less intentional. The *arena of actors* specifies whether power is wielded in dyads or by collectives. Combining these two dimensions yields a four-category typology that incorporates many of the types of power observed in GVCs: *bargaining, demonstrative, institutional* and *constitutive power* (Dallas et al, 2019). Bargaining power (dyadic, direct) operates on a one-to-one basis, exhibits different degrees in different kinds of value chain linkages, and is shaped by the relationship between lead firm requirements and supplier competencies, including those on sustainability. Demonstrative power (dyadic, indirect) operates through informal transmission mechanisms along GVCs between individual actors (such as buyers and suppliers or aspiring suppliers) and is shaped by conventions and best practices, including those on sustainability management, that are implicitly accepted by the parties of a dyadic transaction. Institutional power (collective, direct) operates through government regulation and/or multi-stakeholder sustainability initiatives or other institutionalised forms, and can be leveraged through collective standards or codified 'best practices'. Constitutive power (collective, indirect) is based on broadly accepted norms, conventions, expectations and best practices (financialisation, just-in-time supply chain management, environmental stewardship) and shapes what is systemically acceptable and desirable (green capital accumulation, sustainability-based value extraction from suppliers) (Dallas et al, 2019).

In the rest of this chapter, I examine the intersections of governance and power in the GVCs for coffee and biofuels to highlight the possible mechanisms and strategies that public orchestrators can use to shape environmental outcomes for the public good.

Empirical insights from the coffee and biofuels GVCs

In this section, I draw from the analysis of power, governance and upgrading in the coffee and biofuels GVCs carried out in more detail elsewhere (Ponte 2019) to examine how governments and international organisations could combine a variety of orchestration instruments in different GVCs – depending on their governance structures and the power dynamics that underpin them. In order to develop a portfolio of strategic choices that public actors can use to successfully orchestrate sustainability in different GVCs, I address three questions in the following discussion: (1) how can orchestrators choose what kinds of directive and facilitative instruments to use, and with what balance? (2) how can they enhance issue visibility? And (3) how can they better align private and public sector interests?

Coffee

The coffee GVC was characterised by high concentration at the key nodes of trading and roasting for decades until the late 1990s. However, the degree of concentration at the roaster level has now decreased. In 1998, the top five roaster groups controlled 69 per cent of roasted and instant coffee markets. By 2014, their share had decreased to 50 per cent (Grabs and Ponte, 2019). This is not surprising, given the growth of specialty coffee and the ongoing fragmentation of consumption channels and offerings. However, there have been recent signs of increased merger and acquisition (M&A) activity, which are leading to renewed concentration. In the next sub-sections, I examine the dynamics of different kinds of power in the coffee GVC (drawing from Ponte, 2019) to then return to the issues of GVC governance and orchestration.

Bargaining power

Historically, bargaining power in the coffee GVC had been heavily shaped by institutional power dynamics under an international regulatory regime that lasted from 1962 to 1989. Under the International Coffee Agreement (ICA) regime, collective power relations were relatively balanced between producing and consuming countries, thus strengthening the bilateral bargaining power of suppliers, farmers and their cooperatives. The end of ICA led to a general weakening of bargaining power by producing countries and their producers. In the following three decades, the increasing concentration in the roasting and trading functions of the coffee GVC compounded this dynamic. Despite the relative fragmentation of the roaster segment of the coffee GVC in recent decades, and the continuing consolidation in the international trader segment, mainstream roasters have maintained their upper hand in terms of bargaining power over other GVC actors (see Figure 3.1).

Overall, sustainability content has become more important as major roasters now require third-party sustainability certifications for an important proportion of their purchases. But other roasters have been developing their own sustainability verification systems, which allow them to obtain precious information on suppliers' cost structures as well, thus strengthening roasters' bargaining power and ability to extract value in higher-margin markets. These dynamics suggest that the distinction between mainstream and specialty coffee markets is becoming less clear-cut. Thus, while specialty coffee actors have been taming some of the bargaining power of mainstream roasters, a powerful reaction by major roasting groups is under way, in view of regaining a better bargaining position.

Demonstrative power

Up to 1989, mainstream roasters were mainly focused on selling large quantities of relatively homogeneous and undifferentiated blends of mediocre to poor quality. But later demonstrative power started having an impact with the emergence of specialty coffee. In this context, Starbucks and other 'pioneer' roasters in the US West coast had a massive demonstrative effect in the industry by inspiring a large number of other smaller roasters and café chains. Until the early 2000s, traditional roasters remained slow in responding to the demonstrative power that was sweeping the specialty and sustainable coffee market. But a new phase started, when Procter and Gamble, in response to direct shareholder pressure, announced major purchase agreements to source fair trade coffee. Through a domino effect, Kraft and the Rainforest Alliance then announced a multi-year arrangement in 2004. Albert Heijn and other large European supermarket chains started requiring Utz certification for a portion of their purchases. Since then most of the major coffee roasters have been purchasing considerable amounts of certified sustainable coffee and have adopted their

Figure 3.1: Interactions of different kinds of power in the coffee global value chain

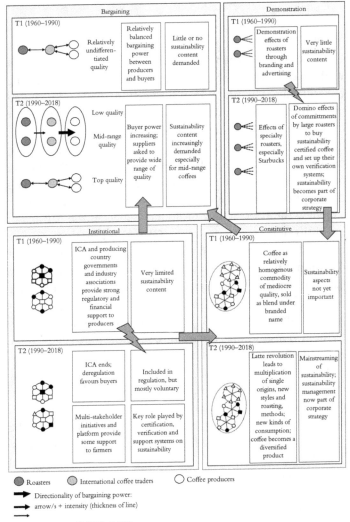

Source: Ponte (2019: 129)

own sustainability standards and verification systems. One after another, they have also acquired smaller specialty roasters and café chains.

Institutional power

Coffee was one of the first commodities for which control of world trade was attempted, starting in 1902 in the Brazilian state of São Paulo. The first ICA was signed in 1962 and included most producing and consuming countries as signatories. Under the ICA regulatory system (1962–89), a target price (or a price band) for coffee was set, and export quotas were allocated to each producer. Although there were problems with this system, most analysts agree that it was successful in raising and stabilising coffee prices. This all changed in 1989, when the US refused to renew the ICA, which profoundly affected the balance of institutional power in the coffee GVC. In turn, this reshaped bargaining power between individual operators to the benefit of consuming country-based actors (including their agents based in producing countries) and to the detriment of coffee farmers, local traders and producing country governments.

While during the ICA period sustainability issues rarely featured in institutional discussions, since the mid-1990s coffee has seen a proliferation of sustainability standards, certifications and verification systems. This has been accompanied by the growth of a large industry of standard developers, certification and accreditation agencies and related service and consulting outfits, which have an embedded interest in the continuing operation of sustainability certification initiatives. The emergence of these systems suggests that institutional power, originally exerted by governments in producing and consuming countries, is now partially wielded by transnational sustainability initiatives.

Constitutive power

Key changes in constitutive power in the coffee GVC relate to the emergence, since the early 1990s of new consumption patterns, the growing importance of single origin coffees, the proliferation of café chains and specialty shops, and increasing out of home consumption. It is against the background of these changes that the specialty coffee industry emerged. This included the proliferation of sustainability standards and certifications (promoted by Rainforest Alliance, Conservation International and Oxfam).

However, in more recent years, and particularly in the past decade, sustainability has become a vector of quality management and supply chain risk minimisation. This has led to a relative weakening of third-party certification and an increasing acceptance in the industry of basic guidelines, company-owned verification systems, and CSR-like projects in coffee producing communities. In sum, sustainability has found an important place in the exercise of constitutive power in the coffee GVC, but in forms that have moved away from more genuine concerns with producers and their environment and towards corporatised forms that are designed to ensure risk minimisation and profit maximisation for roasters, thus enhancing their bargaining power (see Figure 3.1).

Orchestration

In the coffee GVC, governance moved from being multipolar in 1960–90 to being unipolar in 1990–2018, with bargaining power increasing dramatically in the hands of coffee roasters (see Table 3.1). This transition took place through a major change in institutional power with the end of the ICA system. A more recent period of upheaval emanated from the demonstrative power of sustainability and specialty coffee industry actors, which led to a relative dampening of bargaining power by mainstream roasters until recently. This process, however, is now being reversed as mainstream roasters acquire smaller, specialty roasters, and as some specialty roasters have grown to become more mainstream in their operations and procurement systems. Sustainability issues have been an important component of these power dynamics. But what do

Table 3.1: Changes in power, sustainability and global value chain governance in coffee and biofuels

GVC	Polarity (T1)	Changes in bargaining power (T1 to T2)	Changes in other kinds of power (T1 to T2)	Role of sustainability factors in shaping governance (T1 to T2)	Changes in GVC governance (T1 to T2)	Polarity (T2)	Lead firms (T2)	Intensity of bargaining power wielded by lead firms (T2)
Coffee	Multipolar	From balanced to more buyer power	Institutional ++ Demonstrative +	Significant	Major shock in institutional power (end of ICA) together with increasing concentration moves GVC governance from multipolar to unipolar and buyer-driven (by roasters); demonstrative and constitutive power effects of specialty and sustainable coffee initially tame buyer-drivenness; more recently, roasters re-strengthen unipolarity through M&A of specialty	Unipolar	Roasters	High

(continued)

Table 3.1: Changes in power, sustainability and global value chain governance in coffee and biofuels (continued)

GVC	Polarity (T1)	Changes in bargaining power (T1 to T2)	Changes in other kinds of power (T1 to T2)	Role of sustainability factors in shaping governance (T1 to T2)	Changes in GVC governance (T1 to T2)	Polarity (T2)	Lead firms (T2)	Intensity of bargaining power wielded by lead firms (T2)
					operators, sustainability mainstreaming and quality portfolio widening			
Biofuels	Multipolar	Remains relatively balanced	Constitutive ++ Institutional +	Essential	Institutional power plays major role in industry formation; major change in constitutive power recasts legitimate biofuels as only those that are certified sustainable; no major changes in overall governance, which remains multipolar, but blenders and 2nd generation biofuel producers strengthen their position	Multipolar	n/a	n/a

Source: Adapted from Ponte (2019: 131)

these observations entail in relation to public orchestration for sustainability?

Given that the ICA regulatory role is unlikely to be restored, it is public authorities at the national level in producing and consuming countries that could play a sustainability orchestration role in the coffee GVC by exerting their institutional power. Further improvements can be stimulated in combinatory efforts, issue visibility and interest alignment (see Table 3.2). In relation to *combinatory efforts*, both consuming and producing countries can further ramp up many of the facilitative efforts they are already carrying out to support producers, cooperatives and exporters that are seeking voluntary certifications. Producing countries could also include sustainability considerations in national branding efforts, and consuming countries could lobby to raise the low level of sustainability standards currently embedded in some of the basic standards programmes (such as the Common Code for the Coffee Community, 4C). In terms of directive efforts, producing countries could set a minimum sustainability standard for export, charge a sustainability export tax at times of high international prices, and/or include sustainability standards in indications of geographic origin. Consuming countries could more forcefully enact demands for sustainable coffee certification for public procurement (for example in schools and hospitals) and/or require sustainability standards to be imported – as the WTO has been relatively open and lenient in accepting the protection of the environment and health as legitimate policy objectives.

Improving environmental *issue visibility* in the coffee GVC is a more complex challenge. Coffee stories, labels and certifications are already dotting the packaging landscape that speaks directly to consumers. The demonstrative power of specialty and sustainable coffee has been key in partially limiting the bargaining power of mainstream roasters in recent decades. Thus, one idea is that orchestrators could reinvigorate demonstrative (and eventually constitutive) power in alliance

Table 3.2: Overview of orchestration options in coffee and biofuel global value chains

	Coffee	Biofuels
Changes in GVC governance	From multipolar to unipolar	Remained multipolar
Key kinds of power that interacted with bargaining power	Institutional, demonstrative	Constitutive, institutional
Key public orchestrators of sustainability	National governments	National governments, EU
GVC pressure points for orchestration	Mainstream roasters, specialty coffee actors	Multiple
Current level of orchestration effort	Medium	High
Change needed in *combinatory* efforts	From medium to high	Only marginal improvements needed
Possible directive instruments	*Consuming countries*: public procurement; raising the low bar set by 4C; require sustainability certification for coffee to be imported *Producing countries*: require a minimum sustainability standard for export; charge a sustainability export tax	Calling for minimum standards on the quality of governance in private certification systems that are recognised by the EU

(continued)

Table 3.2: Overview of orchestration options in coffee and biofuel global value chains (continued)

	Coffee	Biofuels
Possible facilitative instruments	Further support producers, cooperatives and exporters seeking voluntary certifications; embed sustainability in national branding efforts	Assess impact of sustainability certifications on actual outcomes; further support the scaling up of next-generation biofuels
Change needed in issue *visibility*	From medium to high	Only marginal improvements needed
Approaches to improve issue visibility	Shape demonstrative power by engaging with (smaller) specialty coffee roasters to include, for example, carbon sequestration as part of sustainability and/or minimum farmer prices for meeting specific environmental standards; facilitate initiatives in producing countries that seek to frame sustainability as part of geographic origin and/or national branding	Shape constitutive power to strengthen the framing of sustainability in biofuel production, for example, by facilitating a better incorporation of indirect land change use (ILUC) in calculations of greenhouse gas emission abatements
Change needed in *interest alignment*	From medium to high	From medium to high
Approaches to improve interest alignment	*Producing countries*: charging a mandatory sustainability export tax at the export level to be returned to farmers meeting these standards	Long-term transition measures to facilitate a smooth transition away from first-generation biofuels in order to better align the interests of different groups within the private sector, as this also improves the alignment of private and public interests

Source: Adapted from Ponte (2019: 204–205)

with (smaller) specialty coffee roasters in view of including, for example, climate change and carbon sequestration as part of sustainability. They could also promote efforts to pay a minimum price at the farmer level for coffee that meets certain environmental criteria. Initiatives in producing countries that seek to frame sustainability as part of geographic origin and/or national branding can act in this direction as well. Finally, in relation to *interest alignment*, orchestrators could charge a mandatory sustainability export tax to be returned to farmers. This would provide more direct sustainability incentives at the farm level, as well as better align public and private interests in producing countries – given that many producers perceive sustainability as an imposition placed by buyers and abetted by their governments.

Biofuels

Three systemically important countries/regions are key in understanding the biofuels GVC: Brazil, the US and the EU. Together with Argentina and Indonesia, they account for 90 per cent of global production, and together with China and Canada for 44 per cent of consumption. Global biofuel production and consumption increased nearly seven-fold since 2000 and doubled since 2007. National (Brazil, US) and regional (EU) biofuel industries have existed for decades and have operated fairly independently from each other, indicating that until recently there were a variety of loosely coupled biofuel value chains. In the last two decades, however, we have witnessed a gradual establishment of a *global* biofuel value chain.

Bargaining power

With the exception of Brazil, substantial developments in the biofuels GVC can be traced to the last two decades. International alliances in the private sector and an increasingly complex web of cross-regional investments have emerged in the biofuels GVC, starting tentatively during the 2000s and spreading dramatically during the 2010s – in terms of size, number and geographical spread of international joint ventures and the new involvement of global agro-food traders, oil majors, auto manufacturers and the aviation industry in biofuels (Ponte, 2014).

The global players involved in some of these investments exert dramatic bargaining power in other GVCs, but are still relatively new to biofuels, or had previously played only a marginal role in it (see Figure 3.2). Several global agro-food traders have developed major interests in biofuels. These processes have often led to increased vertical integration in the industry, in order to secure supply, control costs to maximise returns, and ensure processes and sources of supply of certified sustainable biofuels for the European market. This means that bargaining power is still fairly balanced among different kinds of actors in the biofuels GVC, although blenders/distributors have gained some traction by being able to demand sustainability certification in markets where regulation requires it, and by passing on the implementation costs upstream to the producers of feedstock.

Demonstrative power

The flurry of new investments that took place in the past two decades suggests an important role for demonstrative power, as corporations that compete in other industries entered the biofuel craze and mimicked consortium and joint venture models from each other. This involved a disparate combination of actors in the automobile, aviation, biotechnology and energy industries. Demonstrative effects are also evident among major oil companies, which are also investing in biofuel research, in ethanol production facilities and/or in integrated distribution of fuels. Aircraft manufacturers, major global airlines and the US Navy are carrying out projects for the production of 'drop-in' biofuels for aviation. Developers of GM crops are working on feedstocks dedicated to biofuels, also through cooperation agreements with global agro-food traders. In sum,

Figure 3.2: Interactions of different kinds of power in the biofuels global value chain

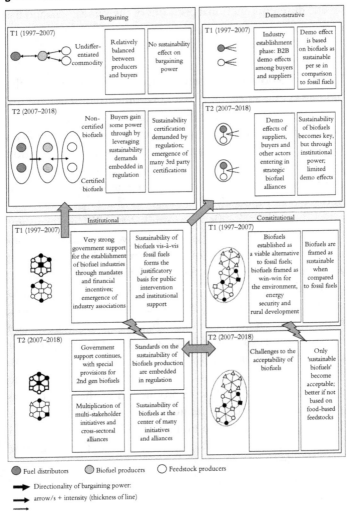

Fuel distributors ●   Biofuel producers ●   Feedstock producers ○

Directionality of bargaining power:

arrow/s + intensity (thickness of line)

Source: Ponte (2019: 130)

demonstrative power is clearly at play in the biofuels GVC, but differently from coffee, it has been wielded by players in several different functional positions of the value chain and has been underpinned in no small measure by government support.

Institutional power

Institutional power is key in understanding the dynamics of the biofuels GVC. Since the 1990s, governments in Brazil, the US and the EU have been heavily promoting biofuels, often under pressure from industry and agricultural lobbies. These policies have been justified in relation to climate change mitigation (especially in the EU), energy security (especially in the US) and farmer support and rural development (in Brazil, but also in the US and the EU).

From the late 1990s to around 2006/07, government interventions enacted policies that effectively forged the various national and, in the case of the EU, regional foundations of an increasingly global biofuel value chain. But as criticism mounted on biofuels (see under 'Constitutive power'), the EU enacted demands for sustainability standards for the production, trade and use of biofuels in member countries. The US also fine-tuned its subsidies and regulation to increase support for next-generation biofuels relative to first-generation biofuels. And Brazil increased its public relations effort aimed at showing that sugarcane-based ethanol production in the country has a positive impact on greenhouse gas emission reductions. Thus, sustainability in the biofuels GVC has become a 'must have' feature in main consumption markets. This is because sustainability standards play a key role in the basic definition of its tradability and are thus a key feature of institutional power dynamics.

For example, the EU promulgated the 2009 Renewable Energy Directive (RED) (2009/28/EC), which required 20 per cent of energy use in the EU and 10 per cent of transport fuels to come from renewable sources by 2020. It also set sustainability requirements for the use of biofuels in the EU, including minimum greenhouse gas savings in comparison to fossil fuels and the double counting of credits for biofuels produced from waste and residues to decrease the impact on feedstock that can be used for food. The Commission set up an accreditation system for private certification schemes that meet its RED sustainability criteria, which has led to a veritable scramble in getting access to the captive EU market. Much of this market has been captured by one particular certification system, ISCC – International Sustainability and Carbon Certification. This means that part of the strong institutional power wielded by public authority has been transferred to private certification organisations that are in charge of verifying compliance with the RED directive.

Constitutive power

In the early days of the biofuel industry, an unusual coalition of agricultural, environmental and military interests, together with a vibrant biofuel conference circuit, exercised constitutive power by establishing the idea that biofuels could achieve a number of collective objectives: revitalise rural areas, decrease CO_2 emissions, and ensure domestic energy independence. This perfect storm also facilitated the institutional support that further stimulated the expansion of this industry. However, increasing food prices and the related food riots of 2006/07 dramatically altered this picture in following years. Civil society groups and researchers started holding biofuel production as a major cause of increasing food prices because it takes land and water away from food production. Many studies highlighted deeply problematic aspects of land investments. Doubts also started to be cast on the impact of biofuel production on greenhouse gas emission reductions. The contours of what is generally seen as 'sustainable biofuel' have changed through these debates. Constitutional and institutional elements of power have been feeding each other in the past decade – with regulation tightening the conditions what is considered acceptable in relation to sustainability (indicated by more support placed on second-generation biofuels), and with constitutive power dynamics playing out in the global biofuel conference circuit (Ponte, 2014).

Orchestration

In the *biofuels* GVC, we did not observe major changes in the multipolar nature of governance in the past two decades or so (see Table 3.1). However, important changes took place in the overlap of different kinds of power, which has key implications for orchestration strategies. Institutional power played a major role in the industry formation period, and bargaining power remained fairly equally distributed among multiple groups of firms in different functional positions. It was a major shift in constitutive power, following the food price crisis of the mid-2000s, that recast biofuels as acceptable only when they are certified or verified as sustainable.

Orchestrators, such as the EU and the US, have already carried out important *combinatory efforts* to seek improvements in sustainability, including substantial directive and facilitative measures (see Table 3.2). However, there is still margin for improvement. For instance, private certification systems that are recognised by the EU to meet its RED directive vary widely, thus calling for minimum standards on governance processes; and the impact of sustainability certification needs to be assessed in view of actual outcomes on the ground. Given that changes in constitutive power dynamics led to a major reshuffling of regulatory instruments, the same could be leveraged to improve *issue visibility*. Orchestrators could, for example, promote a more open debate and consideration of indirect land use change use in the calculations of greenhouse gas emissions abatement in biofuel production. Finally, orchestration measures that are strengthening the position of second-generation feedstock and biofuel producers vis-à-vis first-generation operators should include long-term transition measures to facilitate a smooth transition away from first-generation biofuels, thus improving the overall *interest alignment* between the public sector and different segments of the private sector.

Conclusion

The current fragmentation of sustainability governance entails the need for public authorities to act as orchestrators – by combining directive and facilitative instruments. However, we still do not know the effectiveness of these actions in the context of the everyday practices of lead firms and other actors in GVCs, even though this system of economic organisation has become a dominant feature of the global economy in the past few decades. In this chapter, I proposed three possible enabling factors that can help orchestration to succeed in addressing sustainability issues along GVCs: combinatory efforts including both directive and facilitative instruments; high issue visibility; and interest alignment between public and private actors. While environmental improvements led by GVC actors are most likely to take place in unipolar GVCs (Lister et al, 2015), public orchestration tends to be more successful in multipolar GVCs.

Although improving the chances of successful orchestration involves appropriate combinations of directive and facilitative instruments, ways of enhancing issue visibility and tools to better align private and public sector interests, possibly also across jurisdictions, these choices and strategies are issue- and GVC-specific and cannot stem from a general model of orchestration. They have to be informed by the specific power and governance dynamics that characterise relevant GVCs. This entails targeting appropriate leverage points along a GVC with the right instruments, depending on the balance of bargaining power among different actors and on whether this balance is (or has been) underpinned or challenged by various overlaps of demonstrative, institutional and constitutional power.

In conclusion, for public orchestrators regulation remains essential, but the scale and complexity of the problems at hand require governments and international organisations to use a combination of tools, direct and facilitative, in view of enhancing the visibility of the environmental issues that are more hidden, and of providing incentives and infrastructure to align private and public interests. This requires an understanding of how GVCs are governed and by whom – and the power dynamics that facilitate these processes. Orchestrators need to act not only through their institutional power, but also through shaping constitutive power through ideational change and demonstrative power through collaboration with key influential actors in view of taming the bargaining power of lead firms.

References

Abbott, K.W. and Snidal, D. (2009) Strengthening international regulation through transmittal new governance: overcoming the orchestration deficit, *Vanderbilt Journal of Transnational Law*, 42: 501.

Dallas, M.P., Ponte, S. and Sturgeon, T.J. (2019) Power in global value chains, *Review of International Political Economy*, 26: 666–94.

Gereffi, G., Humphrey, J. and Sturgeon, T. (2005) The governance of global value chains, *Review of International Political Economy*, 12: 78–104.

Grabs, J. and Ponte, S. (2019) The evolution of power in the global coffee value chain and production network, *Journal of Economic Geography*, 19: 803–28.

Horner, R. (2017) Beyond facilitator? State roles in global value chains and global production networks, *Geography Compass*, 11: e12307-n/a.

Lister, J., Poulsen, R.T. and Ponte, S. (2015) Orchestrating transnational environmental governance in maritime shipping, *Global Environmental Change*, 34: 185–95.

Ponte, S. (2014) The evolutionary dynamics of biofuel value chains: from unipolar and government-driven to multipolar governance, *Environment and Planning A,* 46: 353–72.

Ponte, S. (2019) *Business, Power and Sustainability in a World of Global Value Chains*, Zed Books.

Schleifer, P. (2013) Orchestrating sustainability: the case of European Union biofuel governance, *Regulation and Governance*, 7: 533–46.

FOUR

Trade policy for fairer and more equitable global value chains

Louise Curran and Jappe Eckhardt

Introduction

Today's GVCs operate in a very different context to the late 20th century when the concept was first developed. With the recent rise in populism, new tariffs are changing cost structures and thus the geography of several GVCs. Many commentators link this rise in protectionism to concerns about the spread of GVCs and the 'fairness' of competition between countries with very different labour and environmental standards (Rodrik, 2018). At the same time, civil society in many countries is increasingly critical of trade agreements and there are calls for the re-assessment of their governance, especially in order to ensure a stronger voice for labour and the environmental movement (see FoE, 2018, for a recent summary of some of the key proposals of European civil society). In this context, it seems indispensable to reform the system of policy making and implementation to address these criticisms and make trade policy more responsible.

Achieving a 'fairer' global trading system will require a mix of measures – some national, some EU level and some subject to bilateral and multilateral negotiations. In this short chapter, it is not possible to cover all of them. Rather we will focus on the EU level, particularly in relation to its trading relations with developing countries. In the trade policy arena, the EU sees itself as a progressive power, favouring responsible business (Hogan, 2020). It is thus incumbent on it to seek progressive solutions that could subsequently be multilateralised. If the EU can more effectively leverage its trade policy to encourage trading partners to adopt domestic regulation that better protects workers and the environment, it would complement national and EU level regulation, which increasingly requires companies to pay greater attention to negative externalities from their corporate strategies along their supply chains (Hogan, 2020).

This chapter will explore the key areas of EU trade policy where new approaches, or more effective implementation of existing trade regimes, could secure meaningful change. It will focus on those areas where there is the potential for policy shifts in the relatively short timescale of this Commission (up to 2024), rather than more systemic radical change. We will explore the policy options through which trade between EU countries and their partners can be made 'fairer'. Drawing on academic literature, civil society position papers and interviews, we will highlight potential trade policy reforms which could be mobilised to limit the potential negative social and environmental impacts of trade. Our focus on trade policy is, almost by definition, an approach which is primarily focused on influencing behaviour at the state level, although such policy change is often aimed at changing the behaviour of private actors within GVCs. Beyond trade policies, there are many complementary measures which focus on influencing company strategies, such as tax avoidance and due diligence. These are addressed elsewhere in this book.

Setting the context

In any discussion on trade policy options, it is important to note that membership of the WTO implies certain commitments which shape, and indeed constrain, the policy options available to the EU. In the context of promoting fairer trade, countries are not allowed to discriminate between similar members and products. Specifically, they cannot provide different market access to countries 'where the same conditions prevail' or to 'like products'. There are exceptions to these general rules, including for environmental objectives and there is a wealth of WTO jurisprudence which informs the flexibilities on these issues within WTO rules.

In terms of discrimination between similar countries, the EU has lost several cases at the WTO which inform its position, most notably in relation to its banana regime for certain developing countries (where some countries faced high tariffs whereas others were duty free[1]), and its former 'Drug GSP' special access programme. The Drug GSP ruling in particular is significant, in that the EU lost the case not on its right to provide special market access to certain developing countries, but on the fact that it only provided access to countries which were considered to be taking action to address the global drug trade. The subjective nature of this criteria was a key reason that the regime failed to pass legal scrutiny (Shaffer and Apea, 2005).

Thus, any future improved preferential access programme must ensure that it conforms to WTO requirements in that differentiation between countries is based on objective criteria. The EU has largely integrated this requirement into its current GSP+ programme, which uses criteria based on international treaties and commitments to decide eligibility. Were the EU to revise its market access regime to favour 'fairer' trade, it is likely to seek to avoid discrimination that would be judged unfair under WTO rules. It is not impossible to contravene the rules. The US AGOA programme is not WTO compliant, as it only applies to African countries; however, the US secured a waiver – other WTO countries agreed not to challenge it. However, such waivers are politically challenging and historically have only been accepted if the preferences are provided to small peripheral exporters which pose no major threat to key traders.

On the question of 'like products', in general, WTO members must treat similar products originating from their domestic market and other members in the same way. However, there are exceptions. These include the right to ban or restrict goods made by prison labour, or which offend public morals, as well as the right to incorporate restrictions which are 'necessary' to protect the environment or human health. The latter two exceptions, in particular, are subject to a lot of jurisprudence including on tobacco control legislation (US–Indonesia clove cigarettes, Australia plain packaging) and restricting imports of tuna and shrimp because of concerns on by-catch (the US cases: tuna-dolphin and shrimp-turtle).

The key take-aways from these cases are that members can ban or restrict imports of certain products if there is a clear public interest and the measure is 'necessary' according to objective scientific evidence (plain packaged tobacco). In addition, the means by which the policy objective is achieved cannot be arbitrarily imposed by the importing country (tuna-dolphin and shrimp-turtle), which also cannot arbitrarily discriminate between products which are essentially the same (clove and menthol cigarettes). (See Howse and Levy, 2013, for a legal analysis of several key cases).

The current international trade rules thus make it difficult to provide trade preferences to certain developing countries that are not afforded to others, or to goods which are produced in 'fairer' GVCs, with higher social and environmental standards and more equitable distribution of gains. Although the WTO is in a considerably weakened position due to the US blockage of its dispute settlement body, the EU remains committed to its multilateral rules (Hogan, 2020). It is therefore unlikely that

WTO incompatible measures would be instigated by the EU in order to favour fairer value chains.

The potential to increase WTO flexibilities to enable the favouring of socially responsible and fair trade goods has been discussed in the past. In 1995 the European Banana Action Network launched an intensive campaign calling on the EU to include a specific quota for Fairtrade labelled bananas within its import regime. They report that, in response, the European Agriculture Commissioner indicated that the EU could consider a trade policy that differentiated between like products (Fairtrade bananas and ordinary bananas) if civil society were to mobilise opinion in favour of such a move.[2] Thus, at the time, there was some willingness in the EU to try to push the boundaries of interpretation of Articles III and XX of the WTO. If there had been a favourable political environment among WTO members to do so, this might have resulted in increased flexibilities enabling the differentiation between certain 'like products'. However, this proved not to be the case. In particular, the quashing of the US 'Social Clause' proposal at the WTO Ministerial Conference in Singapore in 1996, due to concerns in the Global South about protectionist motivations, undermined the chances of the social aspects of trade being more effectively integrated into WTO.

In a sense, though, the EU already favours trade from countries which have imposed a minimum level of labour and environmental protection under its GSP+ programme. However, these preferences are provided at the level of the country, not the firm or value chain and civil society considers that the guarantees provided in terms of worker and environmental protection are insufficient. As the rules stand, tariff preferences for Fairtrade or other certified goods would be impossible, unless an argument could be made that this is 'necessary' 'to protect public morals'. The EU won a recent WTO case on its ban on importing seal skin products on the basis of this exception, but it has been rarely mobilised in the WTO.

Given this legal backdrop, the rest of this chapter will explore policy actions to favour more sustainably produced goods which could be instigated within WTO rules, in the relatively short timescale of the current Commission. As indicated we focus on two key policy areas which are particularly relevant to the EU's trade with developing countries: free trade agreements (FTAs) and the preferential trading regime – GSP. In both there is increasing pressure for policy tools which enable the voice of labour and the environmental movements to be taken seriously and thus the potential to secure real advances.

Bilateral agreement: FTAs

A key means by which the EU secures market access to other countries and provides access to its own market is through FTAs. Especially since the beginning of this century, these agreements have sought to address issues of sustainable development and trade, laterally through specific chapters on trade and sustainable development (TSD). Recent EU FTAs go further than previous ones in incorporating these issues into trade relations, yet concerns persist about FTAs enabling the development of trade without adequate guarantees that minimum labour and environmental standards are respected. In recent years, the Commission has begun to take concerns about non-respect of TSD commitments more seriously and business groups, conventionally hostile, have become more open to these ideas. The key proposals which emerge from recent inputs to the debate and their feasibility are discussed.

Making the entering into force of an agreement conditional on ratification and application of a list of conventions

The question of sequencing of commitments has been highlighted in several academic studies, as well as in inputs to EU consultations. The EU already uses a list of international agreements to accord GSP+ status and one idea would be to include the requirement to ratify these agreements (or at least the key ones) in its FTAs. In this context, the EU has already indicated that ratification of future FTAs will be contingent on partners adhering to the Paris Climate Accord, with the EU–Japan FTA being the first to incorporate such a requirement. Extending such conditionality to other environmental and labour agreements, by making the launch or conclusion of negotiations conditional on a partner country having ratified and implemented a certain number of core conventions, is perfectly feasible. In fact, the EU–Japan FTA contains obligations for the parties to make sustained efforts to ratify fundamental ILO conventions.

An issue of concern in this context is that, even if such sequencing is secured, there is often a gap between the ratification of international conventions and their application. There would need, therefore, to be an effective monitoring system to ensure that the commitments on environmental protection and labour standards that are made prior to the signature of the FTA are actually implemented on the ground. NGOs are concerned that implementation will not be effective and that the EU does not have the mechanisms in place to hold partners who do not respect their commitments to account. Key to this issue is the question of enforcement, which we will discuss further.

Concerns about non-respect of international commitments will be particularly high profile in the upcoming discussions on the ratification of the EU–Mercosur FTA. Civil society has long expressed concerns that environmental protection has not been effectively integrated into FTAs. The EU has responded to these concerns by making membership of the Paris Agreement a prerequisite for signing an FTA with partner countries. Yet there are fears that Mercosur countries, especially Brazil, are not respecting their Paris commitments in practice. These concerns contributed to the decision by the French government to appoint an independent committee of experts to evaluate the effect of the agreement on sustainable development.

Their conclusions – that the FTA is likely to increase carbon emissions and deforestation – make the ratification of the accord extremely problematic (Ambec et al, 2020). This debate will be a key one in framing the Commission's position on linking FTAs to environmental objectives.

Making the TSD chapters subject to the same dispute settlement as other parts of the agreement

Formal dispute settlement procedures exist within most FTAs to provide a mechanism for the parties to seek redress in case of non-respect of their engagements. In cases where agreements are not honoured such disputes can lead to the complainant party taking action against the other party. In the EU–Japan and EU–South Korea FTAs there are even specific expedited dispute settlement systems for the car sector, where the EU reserves the right to roll back trade liberalisation if the partner does not respect their commitments on non-tariff barriers.

Many NGOs consider that the credibility of the TSD chapters is undermined by the fact that they are not subject to the same formal dispute settlement system as the rest of the FTA. It is a consistent demand that non-respect of environmental and social commitments be similarly subject to dispute settlement and, ultimately, sanctions (for example, FoE, 2018). This is the approach in the US and there is evidence that their more 'muscular' approach to linking FTAs and labour standards can result in progress on the ground, for example in Vietnam (Tran et al, 2017). However, after an extensive consultation on TSD in 2018, the Commission rejected a sanctions-based approach because of the lack of consensus across stakeholders. Instead they launched a 15-point action plan to improve the TSDs, which includes more assertive use of the existing mechanisms to address non-compliance, including dispute settlement (CEC, 2019).

Within this context, a mechanism is needed to ensure that countries accused of social or environmental 'dumping' can be held to account in a meaningful way. The obvious way to do this would be formally integrating the TSD chapters into the dispute resolution procedures of the rest of the agreement. However, given that this option has so far been rejected by policy makers, a mechanism is needed to trigger 'hard' action, such as monetary fines or reversal of trade preferences for certain, affected products within the existing structures. The current TSD chapters do contain a dispute mechanism, but its utility has not been tested. The EU mobilised it for the first time against South Korea in December 2018 following longstanding concerns about labour rights in the country. A panel was requested in July 2019 (CEC, 2019). How this process pans out in South Korea will be a key test case for its effectiveness, so civil society needs to follow this action closely.

However the process of dispute settlement operates, increasing the role of civil society also seems both feasible and desirable. NGOs are often well placed to observe and report on the negative effects of non-respect for international standards, through their dense networks of activists and members. Better leveraging this resource, by giving civil society a more formal role in the FTA monitoring process, would address a key concern of its many critics and help to increase public confidence that monitoring is open and inclusive. The Commission has provided €3m to support civil society involvement in implementation, while a dialogue with Peru was instigated at the request of NGOs operating in the country.

Addressing enforcement

The proposals can only be effective if they are supported by a system that monitors the extent to which trade partners respect their FTA commitments. Concerns about non-respect have led to the publication of regular reports on the EU's FTAs (such as CEC, 2019) and the creation of a new post in the Commission – the Chief Trade Enforcement Officer (CTEO).[3] In July 2019 the first appointee to the post was announced – Denis Redonnet, who is also a deputy Director General of the Directorate-General for Trade. Having a high level official responsible for enforcement is obviously a positive move. However, the appointee is also responsible for two Directorates, one of which is trade defence. This creates a risk that enforcement efforts are disproportionately oriented towards that area – particularly anti-dumping. As with any institutional innovation, how effective the CTEO turns out to be will depend on how much attention is paid to their activities and the extent to which the wider institution supports their operations. If civil society wants to improve the implementation of commitments across the EU's FTAs, they should advocate for an effective and efficient CTEO.

Addressing the negative distributional effects of trade within FTAs

Meyer (2017) has proposed that the unequal distribution of gains through FTAs could be addressed through the inclusion of an 'Economic Development Chapter' in FTAs, such that redistribution of gains from FTAs are built into the agreement. This proposal would require developed countries to commit to taking action within their economies to mitigate the negative impacts of trade, in contrast to most efforts within FTAs, which tend to focus on requiring developing countries to commit to change. However, the methodological difficulties involved in identifying losses from trade have proved substantial. The EU already has a mechanism – the Globalisation Adjustment Fund (GAF) – to support regions hit by globalisation; however, it has never been fully used. The Commission has already proposed that the criteria for accessing support should be expanded in order to extend utilisation and active engagement of civil society in this debate in order to ensure that the outcome is a system that is both more accessible, and fair.

Preferential access: the Generalized System of Preferences regime

In the context of the EU's unilateral trade policy, the Generalized System of Preferences (GSP) is the main policy tool through which sustainable development (SD) can be encouraged in partner nations and, indeed, within this regime the EU has gone substantially further than in its bilateral agreements to incorporate SD concerns into market access arrangements. NGOs, as well as many Members of the European Parliament (MEPs), are sceptical as to whether the provision of generous EU market access, particularly under GSP+, is being accompanied by real progress on the ground in the beneficiary countries; while the Rana Plaza disaster served to further underscore the negative aspects of break-neck growth in supply chains.

There are calls for a more effective use of the existing EU tools to leverage market access to support SD. There is evidence from ILO programmes that market access linked to core labour standards can be an enabling condition to improve working conditions at factory level, as long as they are combined with monitoring and engagement at local level (Rossi, 2015). Others have noted that a combination of 'carrots' and 'sticks' is required to ensure effectiveness of conditionality (Tran et al, 2017).

A key challenge here is to make the monitoring mechanisms linked to GSP market access more robust and beneficiaries more accountable. There is a substantial literature on the effectiveness of making market access conditional on labour or environmental standards and especially on whether the removal or down-grading of access can stimulate positive policy change (Orbie and Tortell, 2009; Rossi, 2015; Smith et al, 2018). The EU's GSP conditionality has had impacts, but these have been more related to ratification than implementation of conventions. In the latest evaluation of GSP, although some positive impacts of conditionality on certain countries were noted, the authors also concluded: 'in several instances, economic growth and export opportunities did not go hand-in-hand with adherence to fundamental labour and human rights' (Development Solutions, 2018). As a country's decision to change its labour or environmental policies is likely to be the result of many domestic and international factors, isolating the effect of trade measures, is, by definition, difficult, yet inaction in the face of clear infringements of commitments is increasingly difficult to justify politically.

There is already a process by which GSP market access can be removed. The 2012 GSP Regulation foresees that preferences can be suspended for 'serious and systematic violation of principles laid down in the conventions listed in Part A of Annex VIII'. The 15 conventions in this annex cover a variety of rights, including labour standards. Thus, unlike in FTAs, the GSP already incorporates the legal tools for preference withdrawal (Vogt, 2015). Yet NGOs and the labour movement consistently report that the EU has failed to act in cases where they consider suspension to be merited.

The EU's conditionality could be a particularly effective lever in the case of beneficiaries of GSP+ or Everything But Arms (EBA) for Least Developed Countries (LDCs). These countries enjoy substantial tariff preferences, which have had significant impacts on trade in certain goods. In 2007 trade unions in Costa Rica and Europe sought unsuccessfully to launch a case over GSP+ preferences granted to Costa Rica over systematic labour rights violations in the tropical fruit industry. At the time the Commission indicated that the ILO processes should be favoured. More recently, the removal of some preferences from Cambodia for human and labour rights violations is widely seen as a step in the right direction. Although the list of products covered is relatively modest, it comes with the threat of more widespread action if progress is not assured. It has even been welcomed by business groups like amfori, representing EU importers. Preferences for Bangladesh are also under threat due to perceived failures to respect workers' rights and freedom to organise. Four civil society organisations have already complained to the European

Ombudsman that the Commission was failing to act in this case. The Ombudsman's judgment makes clear that action is feasible, even if all other avenues will likely be exhausted beforehand (European Ombudsman, 2020). How the Commission deals with these criticisms in the coming years will be a key factor in mitigating the criticisms of the failure of its trade preference system to incorporate 'fairness'.

Concluding remarks

In this short chapter we have sought to highlight the trade policy areas where more 'progressive' approaches that integrate greater labour and environmental protection can be better incorporated into policy implementation in the short term. In summary, the three debates which are most likely to move the dial on the EU's position on these linkages within the timescale of this Commission are:

- The ratification (or not) of the EU's FTAs with Mercosur and Vietnam and the effective incorporation of commitments on SD in case of ratification.
- Increased pressure on GSP+ and EBA recipients on securing real improvements on core labour standards.
- Mobilisation of the new post of CTEO to monitor the implementation of partner countries' commitments on SD objectives in both FTAs and GSP.

Pressure could be stepped up on these issues in the EU context, through political action at the level of MEPs and the Commission, but also in member states. In this context, it needs to be borne in mind that the removal of tariff preferences from a trade partner will never be an entirely technocratic decision of the Commission services. It is inherently political and there would need to be consensus across the member states that any sanctions were justified.

In addition, although the EU can, to some extent, impose conditionality on unilateral preferences accorded to developing countries covered by the GSP, FTAs are negotiated with its trade partners. Large emerging powers are likely to strongly resist conditionality in their agreements. India, for example has a long history of resisting any efforts to link labour standards – including those of the ILO – to trade. Indeed, this is one of the stumbling blocks in the (now stalled) EU–India FTA negotiations. It seems likely that the EU will encounter similar resistance in Brazil to linking its FTA with key NGO priorities like reversing deforestation. In the face of such resistance the mobilisation of civil society will be vital to keeping SD priorities on the policy agenda both in Brussels and the national capitals and enabling the EU, if necessary, to put these long-term objectives ahead of short-term commercial gains.

Finally, WTO reform is being actively discussed. It is not impossible that the global rules which frame trade preferences could change, for example to create an exception for certain types of goods made in more sustainable ways. However, the Drug GSP case made it clear that discrimination between different developing countries must be based on clear international standards. In the case of fair trade, the lack of such an international or European public standard would be a major barrier to instituting such an exception. In any case, the engagement of academics and civil society with this discussion could provide opportunities to create an enabling environment to encourage more sustainable trade.

Notes

[1] Africa Caribbean Pacific Group (ACP) countries had duty-free access to the EU market, largely for historical reasons, while 'third' countries paid a tariff that was €250/tonne in 1993. After repeated challenges in the WTO this has been reduced over time, finally culminating in the 'Geneva Agreement' of 2009 which secured a reduction in third country tariffs to €75/tonne in 2020. In the meantime, most ACP countries continue to have duty free access, but under free trade agreements.

[2] Letter from European Commissioner Franz Fischler to the European Banana Action Network, November 1995.

[3] The New Commission has announced the creation of the post of Chief Trade Enforcement Officer in the Directorate-General for Trade to ensure that trade agreements are respected.

References

Ambec, S., Angot, J.L., Chotteau, P., Dabene, O., Guyomard, H., Jean, S. et al (2020) *Dispositions et effets potentiels de la partie commerciale de l'Accord d'Association entre l'Union européenne et le Mercosur en matière de développement durable*, Rapport pour le Premier Ministre, www.vie-publique.fr/rapport/276279-effets-potentiels-de-laccord-dassociation-entre-lue-et-le-mercosur

CEC (2019) *Report from the Commission on Implementation of Free Trade Agreements 1 January 2018–31 December 2018*, COM(2019) 455 final, Brussels: Commission of the European Communities.

Development Solutions (2018) *Mid-Term Evaluation of the EU's Generalized Scheme of Preferences (GSP)*, Commission of the European Communities, www.gspevaluation.com/wp-content/uploads/2016/12/Final-Inception-Report_GSP-Evaluation.pdf

European Ombudsman (2020) *Decision in Cases 1056/2018/JN and 1369/2019/JN on the European Commission's Actions Regarding the Respect for Fundamental Labour Rights in Bangladesh in the Context of the EU's Generalized Scheme of Preferences*, www.ombudsman.europa.eu/en/decision/en/126086

FoE (2018) *Setting Course for Sustainable Trade – A New Trade Agenda That Serves People and Environment*, Friends of the Earth Europe.

Hogan, P. (2020) Introductory remarks by Commissioner Phil Hogan at OECD Global Forum on Responsible Business Conduct. 19 May, https://ec.europa.eu/commission/commissioners/2019-2024/hogan/announcements/introductory-remarks-commissioner-phil-hogan-oecd-global-forum-responsible-business-conduct_en

Howse, R. and Levy, P. (2013) The TBT Panels: US–Cloves, US–Tuna, US–COOL. *World Trade Review*, 12(2): 327–75.

Meyer, T. (2017) Saving the political consensus in favor of free trade, *Vanderbilt Law Review*, 70: 985–1026.

Orbie, J. and Tortell, L. (2009) The new GSP+ beneficiaries: ticking the box or truly consistent with ILO findings?, *European Foreign Affairs Review*, 14: 663–81.

Rodrik, D. (2018) Populism and the economics of globalization, *Journal of International Business Policy*, 1(1–2): 12–33.

Rossi, A. (2015) Better Work: harnessing incentives and influencing policy to strengthen labour standards compliance in global production networks, *Cambridge Journal of Regions, Economy and Society*, 8(3): 505–20.

Shaffer, G. and Apea, Y. (2005) Institutional choice in the Generalized System of Preferences case, *Journal of World Trade*, 39(6): 977–1008.

Smith, A., Barbu, M. Campling, L., Harrison, J. and Richardson, B. (2018) Labor regimes, global production networks, and European Union trade policy: labor standards and export production in the Moldovan clothing industry, *Economic Geography*, 94(5): 550–74.

Tran, A., Bair, J. and Werner, M. (2017) Forcing change from the outside? The role of trade-labour linkages in transforming Vietnam's labour regime, *Competition and Change*, 21(5): 397–416.

Vogt, J. (2015) A little less conversation: The EU and the (non) application of labour conditionality in the Generalized System of Preferences (GSP), *The International Journal of Comparative Labour Law and Industrial Relations*, 31(3): 285–304.

PART II

Strengthening the role of people and democracy

FIVE

Civil society action towards judiciary changes in the regulation of global value chains

Marilyn Croser

Introduction

The chapter explores the approach adopted by CORE (renamed the Corporate Justice Coalition in April 2021), the civil society coalition on corporate accountability established in the UK in 1998, with regard to recently introduced and proposed laws which require (or would require) companies to identify, and take steps to manage and mitigate, the human rights risks and impacts in their corporate group and supply chains, and considers the prospects for this emerging trend. The UN Guiding Principles on Business and Human Rights, endorsed by the Human Rights Council in 2011 introduced the concept of human rights due diligence (HRDD), a process by which businesses can assess and manage their impacts on human rights. Since then, references to HRDD have begun to be included in legislative instruments in Europe, at both EU and domestic level.

The chapter addresses the early evolution of these requirements, from measures intended to improve corporate transparency (the EU Non-Financial Reporting Directive and the UK Modern Slavery Act) to laws and legislative proposals which create, or seek to create, specific legal duties for companies with associated civil or criminal sanctions for management failures that give rise to human rights abuses. This latter category of laws includes the ground-breaking 2017 French '*Devoir de Vigilance*' law. The chapter provides an overview of these instruments and the ways in which CORE is assessing the political and social dynamics behind their development and adoption, including the corporate response. It also considers the prospects for similar legislation in Europe and beyond, including the possibility of the inclusion of an HRDD requirement in a future EU directive.

CORE: a civil society coalition pushing for corporate responsibility

For several decades, UK NGOs and trade unions have raised concerns about abuses of human rights, workers' rights and damage to the environment linked to the international operations and supply chains of UK multinational companies. High profile early campaigns focused on changing the practices of individual companies and sectors went alongside discussions about legal accountability for abusive and harmful practices. In the late 1990s, UK civil society groups came together to form the Corporate Responsibility Coalition (CORE) to work collectively to campaign for law reform. The chapter begins with an overview of CORE, then moves into a narrative account of campaigns for mandatory requirements intended to improve corporate transparency via company law and supply chain reporting, including an examination of the shortcomings in monitoring and enforcement. It concludes with a brief discussion of recent developments and future prospects for corporate liability.

CORE is a UK network of human rights, development and environmental NGOs, trade unions, academics and lawyers. CORE advocates for government to set standards to improve UK-linked multinationals' transparency about, and accountability for, human rights and environmental risks and impacts in their operations and supply chains, and to enable victims of corporate abuse to access justice. The network now numbers 56 organisations, from international NGOs with wide-ranging mandates, to micro-organisations working on issues in one country or business sector. Separately, they adopt diverse approaches to changing corporate behaviour, including using public campaigning to target companies directly, supporting communities who are taking legal action against firms and participating in MSIs. As a coalition, they work to influence public policy and law through policy development, parliamentary advocacy and research. Businesses cannot join the coalition; however, CORE does collaborate with groupings which include businesses, such as the Ethical Trading Initiative (ETI), and maintains a dialogue with business associations and individual companies.

Why do CORE's partner groups choose to invest time and energy in a joint network? Firstly, they recognise that speaking with a single, united voice is likely to have impact, either in securing a meeting with a decision maker, influencing the outcome of a government policy consultation or raising awareness among parliamentarians. CORE provides a space for the discussion and development of joint advocacy strategies and policy positions, drawing upon the expertise of its partners. For smaller groups with few resources, CORE offers a means to participate in policy processes that they would otherwise struggle to follow and understand. Rather than attempting to reach consensual agreement of all members every time a public position is adopted, CORE works on an 'opt-in' basis, with partners participating depending on their own mandates and priorities. This reduces time spent on the difficult and fruitless negotiations that can sometimes characterise NGO coalition work.

A creative approach to regulation in a neoliberal policy environment

Over the past 20 years, and particularly in response to the right-wing, deregulatory political context of the past decade, CORE has taken an opportunistic, pragmatic approach to advocacy, working to have draft legislation amended to secure the introduction of corporate reporting requirements on human rights and environmental risks and impacts. In early 2019, spurred on by developments in other European countries, the coalition began a proactive campaign for a new law to require companies to take steps to prevent human rights abuses and environmental harm, and to be held accountable in court if they fail to act. The development, outcomes and prospects of these approaches are discussed in turn.

CORE was founded in 1998 when the newly-elected Labour government announced its intention to review UK company law for the first time in 150 years and started consulting with various stakeholders. A group of NGO policy specialists met informally to discuss if and how company law could be used to improve corporate accountability. At the time, companies were developing and promoting their new CSR strategies and voluntary codes of conduct in response to NGO campaigning, although concerns were already emerging about the efficacy of an entirely voluntary approach.

In 2002, CORE instigated and promoted a Private Member's Bill (a legislative initiative by an individual member of the UK Parliament) known as the Corporate Responsibility Bill, which identified new standards in the areas of corporate reporting, company directors' duties and foreign direct liability for corporate human rights abuses. The Bill was tabled by Linda Perham, a Labour Member of Parliament (MP). Although it did not benefit from a parliamentary debate, it enjoyed widespread cross-party support. More than 300 MPs signed motions supporting the Bill's principles and calling on the government to act. As the company law review process gathered momentum, CORE identified three key policy demands: (1) large and medium-sized companies should have to report annually on their environmental and social impacts; (2) company directors should have a legal duty to minimise, manage and mitigate their environmental and social impacts; and (3) obstacles should be removed to ensure victims of corporate abuse linked to UK companies can access justice in the UK.

The government introduced the Company Law Reform Bill (which became the Companies Act 2006) in late 2005. As it made its passage through Parliament the following year, CORE produced a lobby pack for the general public and over 100,000 people contacted their MP to express support for measures to improve corporate accountability. A parliamentary petition supporting CORE's proposed amendments to the Bill was signed by 225 MPs. A pragmatic decision was taken to narrow down the original campaign demands to the introduction of directors' duties and an associated reporting requirement. The end result of the campaign was the inclusion in what became the Companies Act 2006 of a duty for company directors to promote the success of their companies:

> and in doing so have regard to: (a) the likely consequences of any decision in the long term; (b) the interests of the company's employees; (c) the need to foster the company's business relationships with suppliers, customers and others; (d) the impact of the company's operations on the community and the environment; (e) the desirability of the company maintaining a reputation for high standards of business conduct.[1]

Directors of publicly quoted companies are required to report annually on how they have fulfilled this duty. In 2014, the Companies Act 2006 reporting requirements were elaborated via the transposition into UK law of the EU Non-Financial Reporting Directive (NFRD). This directive, introduced largely in response to pressure from civil society, created a requirement for large companies in the EU to provide information that enables an understanding of the impacts of their activity. This includes disclosure of anti-bribery and anti-corruption matters; a description of any due diligence processes implemented by the company in pursuing policies relating to non-financial matters, and the outcome of those policies; and a description of the principal risks arising in connection with the company's operations including, where relevant and proportionate, a description of business relationships, products and services which are likely to cause adverse impacts in those areas of risk; and how the company manages those principal risks. Where a company does not pursue policies in relation to environmental, employee, social, respect for human rights, anti-corruption and anti-bribery matters, the directors must provide a clear and reasoned explanation for not doing so.

The Transparency in Supply Chains clause in the Modern Slavery Act 2015

A fresh opportunity to strengthen legal requirements for corporate transparency specifically in relation to supply chains came with the UK government's 2013 Modern Slavery Bill. Taking inspiration from the California Transparency in Supply Chains Act (TISA), which requires companies with annual worldwide gross receipts exceeding $100 million doing business in California to disclose information regarding their efforts to eradicate human trafficking and slavery within their supply chains, CORE and its partner organisations worked with anti-slavery and anti-trafficking groups, as well as with the

ETI to persuade government to introduce a similar, enhanced requirement for UK companies via an amendment to the Bill.

Prior to the Bill's introduction, the then Home Secretary Theresa May MP commissioned a group of parliamentarians to conduct an evidence review to inform the content of the legislation. One of the review's recommendations was the introduction of a similar set of requirements to TISA. Yet when the draft bill was published, the only reference to company supply chains was a brief mention in the foreword which stated: 'We [the UK government] will continue to work with businesses on a voluntary basis so they can ensure their workforces and supply chains are not exploited.'

In response, CORE published a joint briefing with the ETI arguing for the Bill to be amended to include a supply chain reporting requirement. A meeting with a group of organisations was convened to discuss advocacy strategy for the parliamentary process, which included working to influence the committee of MPs charged with scrutinising the draft law, drafting amendments and identifying parliamentarians in the House of Lords to table them. The government was ultimately persuaded to amend the draft legislation following a joint letter from ETI and British Retail Consortium members, which argued that legal reform would drive efforts to end worker abuse in supply chains.

What became section 54 of the Modern Slavery Act 2015 requires commercial organisations with an annual turnover of more than £36 million operating in the UK to publish a retrospective annual statement setting out what they have done to ensure that slavery and human trafficking is not taking place in their own operations and supply chains. The term 'commercial organisation' encompasses public sector bodies supplying goods or services, including local authorities, universities and health service trusts. The law suggests – but does not require – that statements include information on: the organisation's structure, its business and its supply chains; its policies in relation to slavery and human trafficking; its due diligence processes in relation to slavery and human trafficking in its business and supply chains; the parts of its business and supply chains where there is a risk of slavery and human trafficking taking place, and the steps it has taken to assess and manage that risk; its effectiveness in ensuring that slavery and human trafficking is not taking place in its business or supply chains, measured against such performance indicators as it considers appropriate; and the training about slavery and human trafficking available to its staff. Statements must be signed off by the organisation's board and published on its website. The requirement covers an estimated 9,000 to 11,000 companies.

Monitoring and enforcement: the missing pieces

The directors' duties in the Companies Act 2006 and the Transparency in Supply Chains (TISC) requirement in the Modern Slavery Act 2015 were the first steps in UK law towards company accountability for human rights abuses and environmental damage, no matter where these impacts occur. They begin to expand directors' responsibilities beyond maximising profit for shareholders, to taking into account employees, workers and others affected by business activities, be it in the companies' own operations or its supply chains. Yet despite their significance, these pieces of legislation have major limitations. Analyses of company disclosures to date under the NFRD (including, by extension, the revised Companies Act 2006) reveals that while most acknowledge the importance of environmental and social issues, they do not include detailed information on key issues and risks in their corporate reports.

Research published by the Alliance for Corporate Transparency (2018) shows that over 70 per cent of companies state a commitment to protecting human rights in their supply chains, but only 36 per cent describe their HRDD process, 26 per cent outline their salient issues and just 10 per cent describe examples or indicators of effective management of those issues. Fifty-eight per cent of companies report information about human rights audits; however, disclosure of audit findings is much less common (25 per cent), as is information on actions taken in response (16 per cent). Just 8 per cent of companies acknowledge the widely known limitations of audits, tragically demonstrated by the 2013 Rana Plaza collapse and many other accidents in audited factories. Twenty-five per cent give figures for the total number of outsourced workers, but less than 5 per cent include these workers in their reporting on equal opportunities, collective bargaining or salaries. Only 10 per cent of companies report on payment, or targets for paying a living wage and very few disclose country-by-country information on region-sensitive issues such as equal opportunities (6 per cent) and freedom of association (10 per cent).

A similar picture emerges with respect to TISC. A CORE and Business and Human Rights Resource Centre analysis of the first 75 company statements found that only nine included information on all of the six areas listed in the Act, while only 19 were signed in accordance with the law. Further research by CORE published in 2017 showed that of 50 major companies sourcing products – including tea from Assam, cocoa from West Africa and mined gold, or operating in sectors known to carry a high risk of modern slavery – almost two-thirds had not included information in their statements on modern slavery risks.

The absence of effective monitoring and enforcement lies behind the poor quality of corporate disclosures. The responsibility for enforcing standards in corporate reports published in compliance with the Companies Act 2006 is delegated by the Secretary of State for Business, Energy and Industrial Strategy to the Financial Reporting Council (FRC), whose main mandate is to regulate auditors, accountants and actuaries. Complaints about company reports can be made directly to the FRC's Corporate Reporting Review Team, but

NGO experience is that public findings of non-compliance with the law are highly unusual and the FRC is failing in its duty to regulate firms.

Legal action against directors for breach of their duties could be an option for shareholder activists seeking to hold a firm accountable for human rights abuses or environmental damage, but this is legally complex and financially risky, as in the event of a company winning the case, the directors could seek to recoup their legal costs from the other party. Shareholders in such a case would also have to demonstrate how they had been disadvantaged by the directors' failure to fulfil their duties. Furthermore, unlike the US, there is no tradition of so-called 'derivative' actions in the UK and, unsurprisingly, no such cases have been brought in relation to corporate abuses in supply chains.

The situation is similar with respect to company disclosures under TISC. The National Audit Office (responsible for scrutinising public spending for Parliament (2017)), Parliament's Public Accounts' Committee and three parliamentarians commissioned by the Home Office (2019) to review the Act have been highly critical of government's hands-off approach to monitoring and enforcing the supply chain reporting requirement. All have highlighted the same issues: an inappropriate reliance on civil society, investors and consumers to monitor corporate compliance; the absence of a publicly available list of companies covered by the law; and that the only possible sanction, an injunction issued by the Secretary of State against a company for failing to publish a statement, has never been used.

From reporting to acting: mandatory HRDD and parent company liability

Current legislative reviews of the NFRD and TISC offer an opportunity to address some of the shortcomings described, but they are very unlikely to expand the requirements beyond reporting. A more ambitious approach is necessary to achieve corporate legal accountability for human rights abuses and damage to the environment in international operations and supply chains. This was the aim of the French NGO campaign started in 2014 which resulted in the adoption of the so-called *Devoir de Vigilance* law three years later. This law establishes a legally binding obligation for the largest French parent companies to identify and prevent adverse human rights and environmental impacts resulting from their own activities, from activities of companies they control, and from activities of their subcontractors and suppliers, with whom they have an established commercial relationship. These companies must publish an annual 'Vigilance Plan', to assess and address these impacts. Liability would apply when companies default on their obligations, including the absence of a plan or faults in its implementation.

Similar campaigns are now bearing fruit across Europe. Draft legal proposals are under consideration in Germany, Switzerland and Austria, and the Finnish government made a commitment in 2019 to bring forward HRDD legislation. In May 2020, the European Commission announced that it intends to introduce legislation on corporate due diligence and directors' duties as part of its sustainable corporate governance agenda, and the German Presidency of the European Council indicated that due diligence is a key political priority for their Presidency. In December 2020, the Council of the EU approved conclusions which included a call for a proposal from the Commission for an EU legal framework on sustainable corporate governance, including cross-sector due diligence throughout global supply chains. Major international companies including Aldi, Unilever, Nestlé and Adidas have expressed their support for this initiative.

CORE's campaign for legislation to require UK companies to take action was launched in 2019. General principles outline that the new law will create a requirement for companies to prevent human rights abuses and environmental damage. Like the *Devoir de Vigilance* law, companies would have to put in place a plan to assess and address their risks, and could be penalised for not doing so. The new law would make access to remedy through civil litigation more straightforward for victims by requiring businesses to provide evidence of measures taken to prevent harms, rather than requiring claimants to provide evidence of a company's negligence, as at present. In the most serious cases, company executives could be prosecuted.

The principles were elaborated through consultation with partner organisations and allies, informed by advice from a technical working group of practising lawyers and legal academics. The overall aim was to develop a proposal at once ambitious and legally feasible, that has the potential to garner support from politicians and businesses. Careful consideration of legal practicalities and political feasibility was required. Echoing the language of the Modern Slavery Act 2015, the principles refer throughout to obligations for 'commercial organisations', rather than for companies, meaning the new requirements would extend beyond the private sector to any organisation with a commercial arm, for instance universities and local authorities. No reference is made to the size of companies in scope, a deliberate decision which gives flexibility and leaves this to be defined at a later stage.

Perhaps the most challenging issue was whether and how to formulate a legal requirement for commercial organisations to respect human rights. As this would have represented a radical departure from UK legal tradition (in which private actors are not considered subject to human rights law, unless they are delivering services on behalf of the State), the decision was taken to propose a requirement for action to be taken to prevent human rights abuses, with liability and sanctions for failure to do so, inspired by section 7 of the UK Bribery Act 2010 which requires firms to act to prevent bribery. The adoption of a 'failure to prevent' model for corporate human rights abuses had been recommended by Parliament's Joint Committee on

Human Rights in 2017, indicating pre-existing, cross-party political support for the idea.

Careful consideration was given to whether companies should be required to publish a HRDD plan. French NGO research has found that compliance with this element of the *Devoir de Vigilance* law is relatively low, and that the quality of plans is generally poor, largely due to ineffective government monitoring and an absence of sanctions. Some organisations were concerned that including a similar requirement in the proposed UK law could result in other aspects of the proposal (on liability, for example) being de-prioritised, with the possibility that the final outcome of any legislative process would be little more than an additional reporting requirement. In the end, the decision was taken to include reference to a due diligence plan, as this was a standard demand of campaigns for HRDD across Europe.

In a significant development, in March 2019 the Global Resource Initiative Taskforce (2020), a business and NGO working group supported by three government departments, recommended the introduction of a mandatory human rights and environmental due diligence requirement for companies which place products linked to deforestation on the UK market. Shortly afterwards, the government launched a consultation on a much more limited proposal that would require firms to publish information to show where key commodities – for example, cocoa, rubber, soya and palm oil – come from and that they were produced in line with local laws protecting forests and other natural ecosystems. The proposal makes no mention of human rights and falls far short of the type of accountability mechanism needed to address abuses in supply chains. CORE responded by calling for the UK to be more ambitious in order not to fall behind other European nations. To date the UK government has rejected these calls and is pressing ahead with the introduction of what it describes as 'due diligence on forest risk commodities', which in reality is a limited transparency requirement.

Alignment across Europe, without Europe?

CORE's pragmatic approach to advocacy has yielded results in the past two decades, contributing to persuading government to introduce mandatory corporate reporting requirements. While significant, to date the potential impact of these requirements has been hampered by poor enforcement. The laws are also fundamentally limited by a lack of obligations on firms to act, rather than merely report. In a more favourable political context, French campaigners pursued a more ambitious strategy and achieved the introduction of legislation which offers the prospect of corporate liability for human rights abuses and environmental damage. CORE, and other civil society organisations in Europe are now calling on national governments and the EU to follow suit.

While early signs from Brussels look positive, without a trade deal that includes a commitment to dynamic alignment, there is no guarantee that the UK will maintain or duplicate current or future standards on corporate reporting, due diligence or liability introduced by the EU. CORE may have to brace for a defence of current standards or risk the UK becoming entrenched as a European safe haven for irresponsible business.

Note

[1] Companies Act 2006, Chapter 46, p 79, www.legislation.gov.uk/ukpga/2006/46/pdfs/ukpga_20060046_en.pdf

References

Alliance for Corporate Transparency (2018) *2018 Research Report: The State of Corporate Sustainability Disclosure under the EU Non-Financial Reporting Directive*, http://allianceforcorporatetransparency.org/assets/2018_Research_Report_Alliance_Corporate_Transparency-66d0af6a05f153119 e7cffe6df2f11b094affe9aa f4b13ae14db04e395c54a84.pdf

Global Resource Initiative (2020) *Final Recommendations Report*, https://assets.publishing.service.gov.uk/government/uploads/system/uploads/attachment_data/file/881395/global-resource-initiative.pdf

Home Office (2019) *Independent Review of the Modern Slavery Act 2015: Final Report*, https://assets.publishing.service.gov.uk/government/uploads/system/uploads/attachment_data/file/803406/Independent_review_of_the_Modern_Slavery_Act_-_final_report.pdf

National Audit Office (2017) *Reducing Modern Slavery*, www.nao.org.uk/wp-content/uploads/2017/12/Reducing-Modern-Slavery.pdf

SIX

Assessing the economic, social and environmental impacts of global value chains as a tool for change

Christophe Alliot

Introduction

Despite a growing consciousness of the social and environmental problems at an international scale, the creation of economic value and short-term profitability tend to remain the central objectives of private and public decision makers. Based on this initial observation, the social cooperative enterprise BASIC (Bureau d'Analyse Sociétale pour une Information Citoyenne) was created in the belief that a lever for change lied in greater awareness and understanding of the link between economic activities and social-environmental issues. BASIC was set up in 2013 as a shared platform to mutualise expertise between academic researchers, civil society organisations and public bodies in order to analyse and question the relevance of current business models, whether at the level of a business sector, a company, a territory or a project, and initiate changes at the level of the societal stakes faced today.

The chapter analyses how BASIC achieves such goals via the generation and dissemination of information, knowledge and tools to understand and measure the impacts of economic activities on society and the planet, so as to stimulate the public debate and foster policy decisions towards an ecological and social transition. BASIC has developed a specific methodological approach in collaboration with academic researchers to analyse value chains, assess their societal impacts and estimate related hidden costs at different scales, from international commodities to local products. So far, the framework has been applied to a number of food value chains (banana, cocoa, tea, rice, shrimps, dairy, beef, fruits and vegetables) as well as textiles (sport brands), publishing and mining products.[1]

The case of BASIC's (2018) recent research on coffee and cocoa, and its subsequent diffusion and use in advocacy campaigning, will be analysed to illustrate the objectives pursued, the choices made, the added value as well as the limits of this approach, its potential effects and the challenges faced.

Information for citizen action: the background

The first reports alerting to the social and environmental risks linked to the globalisation of the consumer society date from the early 1970s (Meadows et al, 1972). Since then, despite the development of awareness on the interlinkages between environmental and social challenges faced at the global level and the growing number of initiatives driven by public decision makers and the private sector, the public is increasingly sceptical about the proposed solutions and their capacity to be up to the challenges. Scientific studies increasingly confirm the extent and the worsening of the environmental damage associated with the 'modern' way of life being mainstreamed all around the world. Pessimistic forecasts of climate change, exposure to pollutants and extinction of biodiversity are regularly exceeded. Based on a pattern of unlimited exploitation of natural resources and ecosystems, as well as increasing production of waste (PNUE, 2011), our economic system, and more globally our model of society, is becoming more and more vulnerable.[2] At the social level, human rights abuses persist, employment and working conditions are increasingly precarious (ILO, 2020), and income inequalities continue to increase in most countries (Clements et al, 2015). Despite these evolutions, alternative models of production and consumption most often remain marginalised by the imperatives of short-term economic profitability and the search for the lowest prices. Whatever the business sector, economic growth is the central objective of companies and states alike, which assume it is the only way to generate full employment and social progress, while environmental issues are subordinated to the 'return to growth', a situation which has been amplified by the economic crisis triggered by the COVID-19 pandemic.

Based on this departure point, the 'Bureau d'Analyse Sociétale pour une Information Citoyenne'[3] (BASIC), a Paris-based research institute, was created in 2012 with the objective of questioning the relevance of established business models and value chains, as well as alternative ones, in view of their impacts on society. Its vision and mission are based on the belief that a lever for change lies in the production and dissemination of knowledge on these issues, so as to stimulate a better informed public debate, and, ultimately, to enable citizens, public authorities and private decision makers to make informed choices that are no longer guided solely by short-term, fragmented economic rationale. BASIC has been set up as a 'cooperative of social interest' by constitution, aiming at developing a shared platform of expertise and building bridges between academics and researchers, civil society organisations, journalists, supporters and its employees.

Operationally, BASIC conducts studies on behalf of – and in partnership with – civil society organisations, public authorities and inter-branch organisations which investigate the following research questions:

- How is value created and distributed from producers of raw materials to end consumers? What proportion of value is captured by each stage in the chain, with what profitability? How is it related to supply and demand dynamics, to governance structures of the chain (negotiation imbalances, power relations, monitoring tools, etc.), to the socioeconomic context of each territory and to institutional settings (public policies and regulations, standards and certifications, etc.)?
- What are the impacts generated by each stage in the chain on society: social, health, environmental, economic? What are the main causes, impact pathways and loops, as well as systemic relationships between impacts and lock-ins? Which indicators enable to quantify their current level and evolution?
- What are the related hidden costs shifted onto society (societal costs)? What is the order of magnitude of real expenses borne by public authorities and third parties as a result of these impacts (when possible/relevant to assess)?
- Based on these elements, what comparisons can be drawn between models of production and consumption? Which ones can address the social and environmental issues at stake and those that should be regulated or replaced?

In order to investigate these research questions, BASIC has chosen to combine qualitative approaches with quantitative methodologies that articulate economic, social and environmental data related to all stages along value chains, from producers of raw materials to end consumers. Its objective is to leverage today's wide availability of quantified data and see how to use them to better inform the public debate, at a moment when quantified information seems to be increasingly used out of context to reassert certain viewpoints and contradict diverging ones. In doing so, BASIC has been confronted with the critical need to understand where data come from, by whom they are collected, with what intention and using which methodological framework, with what limits and biases. These questions are not only relevant to raw data, but also to the models which use them to generate knowledge and recommendations: how are they developed, by whom, and so on? The example of recent studies conducted on coffee (BASIC, 2018) and cocoa (BASIC, FAO and EuropeAid, 2020) GVCs are a good illustration of the issues at stake when developing quantitative methodologies, and possible ways of addressing them.

Mining data or data minefields? The missing information on value chains

The first set of issues relates to the collection and processing of raw data. When doing so, one of the first lessons learnt is the fragmentation of available quantitative information, some important subjects being potentially 'left in the dark' by the lack of data. This can be due either to their complexity, the limited resources dedicated to investigating them, or simply the willingness of some actors not to disclose information. In the case of the coffee global value chain, this is typically the case of the 'out of home' market (for instance, cafes, restaurants, coffee shops like Starbucks) for which very limited data are available when compared to sales in supermarkets and hypermarkets. The main underlying reasons are the high number of business actors involved and the lack of resources – public and private – dedicated to consolidating quantitative information on the 'out of home' sector. In addition, there is a degradation of the availability of public statistics on certain groups of actors and stages of the value chain. A good illustration is the decline in the precision of the economic surveys conducted annually among private companies by the French public statistics institute (INSEE). As a result, private fee-based databases are an indispensable source of information to analyse specific business models of companies, estimate their market shares, and so on.

This situation can be further worsened by the decision of some leading actors not to publish any specific data on their activity, best exemplified by Nespresso which refuses to disclose information on sales in its stores, although its market share on single-serve coffee (capsules) can exceed 35 per cent in consuming countries such as France. This issue can be just as critical at the level of farmers operating at the beginning of the value chain, where key production systems can be under-documented. In coffee, this is for example the case of semi-forest coffee farming systems in Ethiopia, although they are the most common in the country and the way coffee has been produced there for centuries. This lack of information leads to a risk of oversimplifying the real situation of actors by relying on average estimates that do not account for specificities, and creates a critical difficulty when putting raw data in context.

This also hampers the capacity to make connections between the types of information available. For example, in coffee, one of the main difficulties encountered was to quantify the relationship between the price paid to farmers for coffee, and the annual income earned by their households, because of the lack of public information and studies assessing this relationship. Similar difficulties have been faced when trying to identify the proportion of total deforestation that is attributable to coffee farming in key regions (such as in Peru or Ethiopia). In such situations, the main way to overcome methodological obstacles is to conduct additional data collection or to liaise with ground actors who have done so, or are in the process of doing so.

Even when data is available, the other issue that often arises is the contradiction between results from different sources, with often wide discrepancies. In the case of the coffee global value chain, this problem was first and foremost salient regarding estimates of market shares of traders, processors, brands and retailers. Among the relatively scarce data available on this topic – because of its sensitiveness in the business world – contradictions appear to be the norm rather than an exception. This can be explained essentially by differences in scope: even if the sales taken into account for a given actor are the same across estimates, it is the perimeter chosen to calculate the market share that most often differs (for instance, total market sales versus sales only in supermarkets). This problem is not limited to business actors and can be just as important when analysing the agricultural stage of the value chain. In the case of the coffee value chain study, diverging and even contradictory statistics emerged from different data sources claiming to assess the same research questions in the same country or region, with divergences of up to 100% regarding the number of farms, the number of hectares harvested, the yields, the income generated, and so on. As in the case of business actors, these contradictions could be most often explained by major differences in the scope of actors and regions covered by the statistics.

Such contradictions can also derive from the assumptions made to generate data, as illustrated by the results of lifecycle analyses regarding greenhouse gas emissions of different formats of coffee beverages. When comparing coffee made from aluminium capsules and brewed coffee, the emissions can be to the advantage of the former or the latter depending on the study, because of differences in the quantity of coffee considered necessary to make a cup. These findings show the need to collect as many data sources as possible when investigating value chains and their impacts, as assessing the potential contradictions between these sources is the main way of understanding their construct and biases.

Combining quantitative and qualitative approaches

Moreover, greater insights arise when confronting quantified data with qualitative information collected through interviews and literature review. This is why BASIC has chosen to systematically conduct in parallel quantitative and qualitative investigations. When contradiction arise between the two, it either sheds light on new phenomenon/trends thanks to quantitative data or questions the limits of these data thanks to qualitative insights. For example, in the case of the coffee value chain, the collection of quantified information on the additional costs involved in manufacturing capsules (whether made from aluminium or plastic) has shed light on the debate over value distribution in the sector. Indeed, these data have demonstrated that the much higher price paid by consumers for coffee capsules of the Nespresso type (on average five times more expensive per kilo than a usual 250g pack of ground coffee) could not be explained by their additional packaging costs: less than 25 per cent of the additional price to consumers could be related to such costs, whereas most actors thought that it would be closer to 100 per cent, according to the qualitative interviews conducted.

Conversely, qualitative analyses often bring indispensable insights which are not yet quantified, or very poorly, thereby shedding light on the limits and biases of existing data sources. Still in the coffee sector, this was best illustrated by the case of Ethiopian mid to large size plantations that are developing rapidly and competing with the almost 2 million small farmers who are growing coffee on less than 0.5 hectares. Even though these modern specialised plantations are creating unfair competition for small holders and posing new challenges with regards to deforestation and precarious employment, they were not properly covered by national statistics at the time of the study. It is through interviews with actors in Ethiopia and the work of a PhD student from the French Agronomy School AgroParisTech that this important phenomenon could be identified. The phenomenon has yet to be comprehensively quantified in order to better understand its scale and speed of development. The following charts show some of the main quantified findings of the study on coffee value chains performed by BASIC in 2018, notably the evolution of average prices and costs along the chain in France, illustrating the results that can be obtained through the work on data detailed previously.

Figure 6.1 shows the evolution of:

- the total value of green coffee beans imported into France annually;
- the combined added value generated each year by roasters and retailers in France from their sales of coffee, all formats being included: packs of 250 grams, instant coffee, soft pods and capsules (in other words, it is the difference between the total value of consumer purchases of coffee in supermarkets and hypermarkets minus the total value of green coffee beans imported in France); and
- the total costs of roasting and grinding coffee as well as logistics costs and the costs to manufacture packaging, in particular coffee capsules whether in aluminium or plastic.

The results illustrate some of the key tendencies of the whole French market over the past 20 years:

- The total value of coffee beans imported into France has been in the same range in 1994–98 and in 2013–17, with important instabilities in between (reaching a low point of €184 million in 2003 and a peak of €617 million in 2011).
- The combined added value of roasters and retailers has undergone a steady increase over the period which resulted in its doubling from €1,222 million in 1994 to €2,598 million in 2017. This spectacular jump is essentially due to the increasing proportion of coffee capsules sold on the market at five times the price of regular 250g packs of coffee (in 2017, they accounted for 58 per cent of all French sales of coffee consumed at home).
- In comparison, the total processing costs induced in France by roasting and grinding coffee, manufacturing the packaging (including capsules and pods) and shipping the

Figure 6.1: Evolution of the value distribution of coffee products consumed at home, 1994–2017, € million

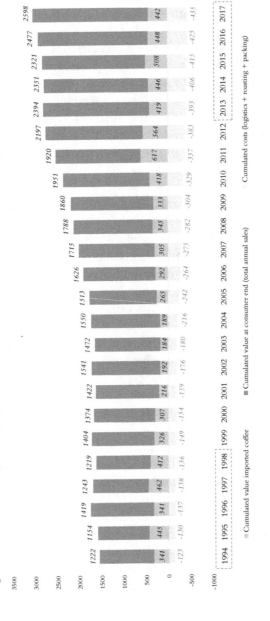

Note: The figures include all formats: 250g packs of coffee, instant coffee, soft pods and capsules of coffee

final products to the supermarket stores has also increased markedly from 123 million euros in 1994 to 435 million euros in 2017, mainly because of the increasing proportion of capsules sold that cost more to manufacture. However, it is important to see that the increase of total processing costs (approximately €312 million between 1994 and 2017) is four times smaller than the increase accruing to combined added value of roasters and retailers (approximately €1,376 million between 1994 and 2017), which indicates a significant increase of net profitability for the actors at the end of the chain.

In contrast, the two charts in Figure 6.2 display the results obtained regarding the average real income earned by coffee farmers in three countries of origin which have been studied in more detail – Peru, Ethiopia and Colombia – and compared with two thresholds: the poverty line and the living income threshold. These findings demonstrate that the situation of conventional coffee farmers has worsened markedly in Peru and Ethiopia over the past 20 years, as they have lost almost 20 per cent of their income from coffee when corrected for local inflation, thereby remaining well below the poverty line (except for 2011 when climatic events induced very significant losses of coffee production in Latin America, which translated into a price spike on world coffee markets, a one-off situation that has benefited bigger farms, but not small holders). The economic situation of coffee farmers in Colombia seems much more sustainable, thanks to the strict and comprehensive public regulation of the sector and heavy investments and subsidies by the state. However, even in this case, the coffee farmers remain globally below the living income threshold (even if they lie above the poverty line on average). Beyond these considerations regarding raw data and their processing, other critical issues concerning quantitative approaches relate to the analytical models that use these data.

Figure 6.2: Evolution of income of coffee growers in Peru, Ethiopia and Colombia, and comparison with the poverty and living income thresholds

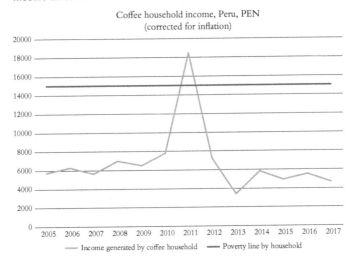

Coffee household income, Peru, PEN
(corrected for inflation)

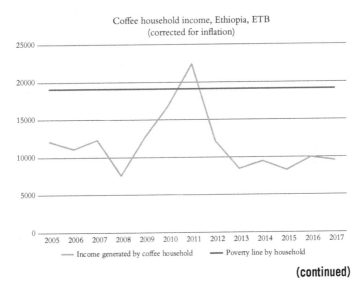

Coffee household income, Ethiopia, ETB
(corrected for inflation)

(continued)

Figure 6.2: Evolution of income of coffee growers in Peru, Ethiopia and Colombia, and comparison with the poverty and living income thresholds (continued)

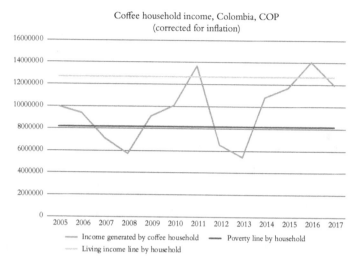

Coffee household income, Colombia, COP
(corrected for inflation)

— Income generated by coffee household   — Poverty line by household
— Living income line by household

The interest of models, but which model?

This is best exemplified by BASIC's (2020) recent study on cocoa value chains published in partnership with FAO and EuropeAid. Among the starting points of this study was the review of the limits of existing studies on price transmission along the cocoa chain, which have mainly analysed this phenomenon through econometric models. These models are first and foremost based on statistical analyses of price data at different stages in the chain, and the definition of mathematical relationships between them. In order to function, these models require the use of information sources offering a large enough array of data to conduct statistical and mathematical calculations. In practice, the econometric models of price transmission we have identified with regards to cocoa are often limited to analysing the dynamics between cocoa farmers and the world market price on the commodity exchange. This is apparently due to the lack of data documenting the rest of the chain and the difficulty, if not impossibility, of relating mathematically the chocolate finished goods with the cocoa farmers producing the beans. Beyond economists and the academic field, most operational actors often consider these models – and the results they provide – as too theoretical.

In this context, BASIC has chosen a different route: the elaboration of a value chain systemic model based on qualitative rather than statistical analyses. This model has been founded on a qualitative understanding of:

- the functioning of end consumer markets, in particular the role played by key categories of finished goods which structure the consumers' demand (because of market segmentation, brand reputation, market share, labels, etc.);
- the business functioning of operators at each stage of the chain (from cocoa farmers to end consumers), in particular regarding their internal costs and margins, and the potential variations depending on types of operators (for instance, small holder or plantation, small-scale or large-scale processors);
- the commercial relationships and price negotiation dynamics between the different operators along the chain, and the potential variations linked to the types of operators; and
- the links between finished goods and the different types of operators along the chain, in order to articulate the previously detailed results.

Based on these, relevant sources of information have been identified in order to feed the model with data. To achieve this, the different issues described earlier regarding raw data have been taken into account, such as collecting as many sources as possible for each data point, cross-checking them to identify contradictions, and confronting them with qualitative analyses to check their relevance. Connecting data to the model has highlighted an additional challenge: as data are most often organised and structured for business purposes, it has required an extra level of understanding of their fundamentals in order to use them meaningfully, and to build some assumptions to compensate for missing information. At the end of the process, qualitative interviews have been conducted with operators from the whole chain so as to confront the results obtained, question the model, amend it and eventually validate it so that the end results are sufficiently sound to make sense for them. In order to keep the results easy to understand from a non-expert view, a didactic tool has been developed. It enables any user to navigate the results, entering gradually into details, and offers a great level of transparency on every estimate (assumptions, sources of raw data, calculations made and their limits), all critical elements to build trust in the results.

Going beyond value distribution

The results obtained through this approach provide first estimates for the distribution of value, internal costs, taxes paid to authorities and net margins along the whole value chain, as illustrated in Figure 6.3 for the case of plain dark chocolate tablets, from the farmers situated in four origin countries (Côte d'Ivoire, Ghana, Cameroon and Ecuador) to end consumers in France. These results demonstrate the clear asymmetry of value creation that exists along the cocoa/chocolate chain: on average 70 per cent of the total value and 90 per cent of the total margins generated from cocoa farmers to end consumers accrue to the two last actors in the chain, brands and retailers. At the beginning of the chain, cocoa farmers only receive on average 11 per cent of the final price, whereas a high percentage of them are living under the poverty threshold, as the most recent World Bank (2018, 2019) estimates reveal in Côte d'Ivoire and Ghana. The model developed shows that the three main factors linked to 'downstream' actors in the chain (retailers and brands) have a very significant impact on this distribution of value, costs and margins:

- the type of brand (national brand Vs private label);
- the marketing mix (basic, cooking, premium); and
- the products' performance (best-selling products, as opposed to other products).

In contrast, all upstream factors analysed (country of origin, percentage of cocoa in the final product, country of first processing) have a quite limited impact, if any, on the distribution of value and costs from cocoa farmers to end consumers. These findings can be largely explained by the fact that the majority of value creation in the chain is linked to

Figure 6.3: Distribution of value, costs and margins of plain dark chocolate tablets in 2018 (cocoa harvest 2017/18)

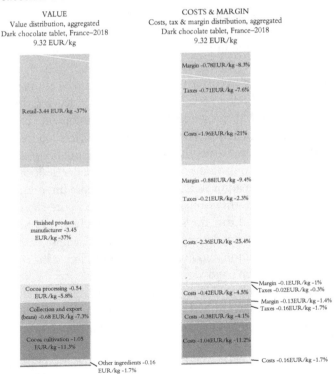

intangible levers (marketing segmentation, brand reputation) which are essentially controlled by brands and retailers, and largely prevail over the territory of origin and the work of farmers. Indeed, consumers appear to rarely value these elements, whereas the percentage of cocoa is seen to matter most and defines the quality of chocolate tablets, as a result of the successful marketing and advertisement campaigns of large brands and retailers. These results illustrate the relevance and interest in investigating the distribution of costs, tax and margins in addition to the split of value among the actors of the chain, as it provides indispensable insights into the functioning of value chains and the strategies of business and public actors.

Supporting transparency for more informed dialogue and negotiation

As presented in the introduction, the aim of this quantitative work performed by BASIC is to better inform the public debate via the creation of sets of data and models that can be ultimately shared among different actors of a given sector, leaving them the room to draw their own analyses and conclusions, but based on mutually agreed data. The long-term idea is to support the creation of a more in-depth dialogue among public, private and civil society organisations, not only on the distribution of value, costs and margin along the chain, but more importantly on the conditions that would enable everyone in the chain to make a living and that the sector as a whole becomes more sustainable, in particular regarding the fight against climate change and pollution, biodiversity protection, living income/ wages, or children's and workers' rights.

First discussions in this direction are being initiated by the European Commission, the FAO, private actors and civil society organisations in the cocoa, coffee and banana sectors. The objective of BASIC's contribution is to continue the questioning and developing its approach and methodologies described in this chapter by:

- discussing it with academic researchers and experts of the sectors analysed;
- extending the scope of products and countries covered, but also the sectors analysed, for example textiles, building on the case study of Zara that BASIC has conducted in partnership with Public Eye and Collectif Ethique sur Etiquette (BASIC, 2019);
- trying to enrich it with the work it has conducted recently on the distribution of value and profits within firms of the CAC 40,[4] and the related corporate governance systems (BASIC, 2020); and
- articulating findings on value distribution with the analysis of social and environmental impacts, and question the business rationale, through the comparison between value created and hidden costs offset on society – as undertaken in the study of the coffee global value chain (BASIC, 2018).

Notes

[1] The results of this body of research are freely accessible at https://lebasic. com/en/our-publications/

[2] The ecological footprint of our production and consumption models has exceeded the regeneration capacities of our planet since the 1970s, and the situation continues to deteriorate (United Nations, 2020; WWF, 2020).

[3] In English: Bureau for the Analysis of Social Impacts for Citizen Information.

[4] The top 40 French publicly quoted companies.

References

BASIC (2018) *Coffee: The Hidden Crisis Behind the Success Story – Study of the Sustainability of the Coffee Sector*, BASIC, https://lebasic.com/ wp-content/uploads/2018/10/BASIC_Coffee-Value-Chain-Study_Research-Report_October-2018_Low-Res.pdf

BASIC (2019) *Etude sur le modèle économique de Zara, la distribution de la valeur dans ses chaînes d'approvisionnement et sa capacité à y assurer des salaires décents*, BASIC, https://lebasic.com/wp-content/ uploads/2019/11/ESE_Le-cout-du-respect-selon-Zara_2019.pdf

BASIC (2020) *Evolution de la répartition de la valeur au sein du CAC 40: données et analyse 2009–2018*, BASIC, https://lebasic.com/wp-content/uploads/2020/06/BASIC_Rapport-Recherche-CAC-40_Juin-2020.pdf

BASIC, FAO and EuropeAid (2020) *Comparative Study of the Distribution of Value in European Chocolate Chains*, FAO, https://lebasic.com/wp-content/uploads/2020/07/BASIC-DEVCO-FAO_Cocoa-Value-Chain-Research-report_Advance-Copy_June-2020.pdf

Clements, B., de Mooij, R., Gupta, S. and Keen, M. (2015) *Inequality and Fiscal Policy*, Washington DC: International Monetary Fund.

International Labour Organization (ILO) (2020) *World Employment and Social Outlook*, www.ilo.org/wcmsp5/groups/public/---dgreports/---dcomm/---publ/documents/publication/wcms_734455.pdf

Meadows, D.H., Randers, J., Meadows, D.L. and Behrens, W. (1972) The limits to growth: a report for the Club of Rome's project on the predicament of mankind, Potomac Associates.

PNUE (2011) *Waste: Investing in Energy and Resource Efficiency*, United Nations.

United Nations (2020) *Millennium Ecosystem Assessment*, United Nations.

World Bank (2018) *Ghana: Priorities for Ending Poverty and Boosting Shared Prosperity (Systematic Country Diagnostic)*, World Bank.

World Bank (2019) *Au pays du cacao: comment transformer la Côte d'Ivoire*, World Bank.

WWF (2020) *Living Planet Report 2020*, https://f.hubspotusercontent20.net/hubfs/4783129/LPR/PDFs/ENGLISH-FULL.pdf

SEVEN

Worker- and small farmer-led strategies to engage lead firms in responsible sourcing

Alistair Smith

Introduction

This chapter draws on the 25 years of experience of a small UK-based NGO, Banana Link (BL), which has played a key role in facilitating and advocating South-led strategies to raise awareness of – and influence solutions to remediate – the negative social, economic and environmental impacts of the production and trade of the world's most consumed fresh tropical product along the value chains from field to consumer (Banana Link, 2020). The approach is proposed as an original contribution to North–South civil society relationships and action along GVCs.

Starting from a world where those at the beginning of the chain were completely disconnected from powerful players at the consumer end of the chain, independent trade unions and small farmers' organisations in banana exporting countries created strategic spaces alongside civil society allies in consumer countries that have enabled them not only to understand the complex landscape of economic and political stakeholders well beyond their immediate fruit company employers, but also to transform this understanding into practical advocacy and influencing strategies designed to change the behaviour of 'lead firms'.

Who are the 'lead firms' in the case of bananas?

The 'lead firms' in banana value chains are no longer the iconic global brands like Chiquita, Del Monte, Dole or Fyffes – creators and perpetrators of the so-called 'banana republics' in Central and South America in the 20th century. Since the 1990s and early 2000s the lead firms referred to here are the major retailers that have accumulated bargaining power sufficient to set the terms of trade back along the chain from farms and plantations. In the 2010s, global retailers, especially those based in Northern Europe, have been increasingly using that buying power to influence the social and environmental conditions of production, packing, transport and ripening. In response to pressure from civil society, retailers are now also starting to use their direct influence through negotiations with suppliers, in a bid to convince consumers of the 'sustainability' or 'responsibility' of their offer.

It was estimated in 2015 that across the EU28 the retail companies took on average 40 per cent of the total value available along the chain (BASIC, 2015), generating in many cases very substantial profit margins on what for most is the single biggest selling food product on their shelves. By 2020, the top ten grocery retailers sell at least one in every two bananas consumed in the EU, the world's single largest consumer market in volume imported and per capita consumption (even after UK withdrawal) (Table 7.1).

Table 7.1: Top ten European lead firms at the top of banana chains, 2020

Lidl/Kaufland (Schwarz group), DE	Retail presence in all 27 EU member states, UK and US
Aldi Nord & Süd, DE	Retail presence in 14 EU countries, UK, CH, US, China and Australia
Carrefour, FR	Present in 6 EU member states, and in 24 other countries on four continents
Tesco, UK	Retail presence in UK and 4 EU member states, and has sold all Asian operations
Edeka Group, DE	Retail presence in Germany (largest food retailer) and Denmark
Rewe Group, DE	Retail presence in 14 EU member states and Ukraine
Metro, DE	Mainly wholesale activities in 20 EU member states, UK, Morocco, Russia and Asia
E.Leclerc, FR	Retail presence (largest food retailer in France) in 7 EU member states
Auchan, FR	Retail presence in 8 EU member states, Russia, Ukraine, Asia and Africa
Intermarché (ITM Group), FR	Retail presence in 4 EU member states

Source: Compiled from trade date and company websites by Banana Link

A very short history of the process of empowerment of organised workers and farmers: consolidating a 'slave-free triangle'[1]

Small farmer organisations that had emerged in the four Eastern Caribbean island states of Saint Vincent and The Grenadines, Saint Lucia, Dominica and Grenada as a result of processes of land reform following independence from Britain came together to form the Windward Islands Farmers' Association (WINFA) in 1982.[2] In the late 1980s some 25,000 farming families across the four countries – with less than two hectares each on average – exported their fruit to the UK under preferential trading arrangements with the former colonial power, shipped by British company Geest, itself created by a 1950 act of Parliament after social unrest in the islands provoked by the collapse of world sugar prices threatened to disrupt British rule.

In the face of the pending harmonisation of trade regimes across the then EU-12 in 1992, farmers' leaders asked Farmers' Link – the small East Anglian NGO that spawned BL – to provide policy information emanating from London and Brussels that would help farmers in the islands design strategies to deal with the 'cold winds of free trade' threatening to do away with the small farmer-based industry that had become the backbone of the Windward Island economies (Thomson, 1987).

The following year, in 1993, after two years of pioneering work by a Costa Rican banana trade union leader to contact his peers from Colombia in the South to Guatemala in the North (by bus), the Latin American Banana Workers' Union Coordinating Body (COLSIBA) was born in San José, bringing the independent plantation-based unions together into a common platform, initially from six countries.

COLSIBA brought together organisations from different political traditions into one body that drew its initial cohesion from the same common concern that had been identified by their Eastern Caribbean small farmer colleagues, the creation of a single European market for bananas. From a plantation worker perspective, the issue was how to deal with the downward pressure on labour costs and therefore labour rights and working conditions driven by the multinational banana companies' jockeying for position ahead of the highly contested EU banana import regime, put in place just weeks after COLSIBA was created.

In 1994, at the instigation of Farmers' Link and the German and Swiss not-for-profit alternative banana trading organisations Banafair and Gebana, the European Banana Action Network (EUROBAN) was founded with NGOs initially from five countries. The network soon grew to include trade unions and NGOs from a dozen countries.

From the outset, the network drew on the political agenda of WINFA and COLSIBA to design its own agenda around two major strategic goals: to build a common South–South–North advocacy presence to secure an EU import regime that was beneficial for both small farmers and plantation workers; and to explore the feasibility of a pan-European fair banana trading initiative.

From the outset, the challenge of aligning the potentially divergent interests of plantation workers and small farmers was key to the strategy of influencing public policymakers, multinational fruit brands and, in due course, the emerging lead firms. Articulating and amplifying the weakest voices in the chain as a single advocacy position, despite the differential impacts of private and public policies on each group, was achieved through systematic and very regular consultation and joint strategising.

In the mid-1990s, an intensive series of quarterly meetings was organised around Europe, facilitated by Farmers' Link then BL[3] in its role as host to the EUROBAN Secretariat. COLSIBA, WINFA and Central American civil society representatives all participated systematically in these meetings (funding permitting), and in the whole process of sharing information, organising public campaigning[4] and political advocacy proposals, feeding into the design of the criteria for the new Fairtrade mark, and engaging policy makers at national and EU level.

This intensive phase of alliance-building generated a common vision for the necessary transformation of the industry around the concept of sustainability in its three core dimensions: social, environmental and economic (Smith, 2010). The need then was to start the process of engagement with the key economic players in the global industry by the South–South–North civil society alliance of organised small farmers, plantation and packhouse workers, and a diverse network of mainly European civil society organisations.

To avoid our agenda being dominated or even determined by more resource-endowed North-based organisations, BL had to argue that the voices of our South-based allies should always be seen as determinant if we were to present a coherent and authentic common position to Northern policy makers on the trade policy issues in particular. The strategy was explicitly conceived to contrast with the divided governmental positions that were in conflict at the new WTO (with the fruit multinationals lobbying overtly to defend their interests: the US and Latin American governments on the one hand, and the Caribbean and African exporting countries on the other). Our policy proposals, such as creating an EU import quota for fair trade bananas, were designed to benefit both small farmers and plantation workers and cut across the geopolitical divide that marked the bitter dispute over the EU import regime.

In order to avoid any recuperation of our common 'sustainability' agenda by private or public institutions, the triangular South–South–North alliance decided we needed to organise engagement ourselves, inviting people to discuss our agenda, on our terms.

Moving up a gear: 1998 to 2005

The civil society alliance – now joined by the global trade union federation International Union of Agriculture and Foodworkers' (IUF),[5] Ecuadorian and Filipino small farmers' organisations and a US labour rights NGO – organised two International Banana Conferences on the themes of 'Towards a Sustainable Banana Economy' in 1998 and 'Reversing the Race to the Bottom' in 2005, both held in the European capital and preceded by a series of regional preparatory seminars. In both cases there was a conference organising secretariat in the North (staffed by BL) and one in the South (staffed by COLSIBA). These major events generated an unprecedented level of participation from a wide range of industry players, partly because of the media's consistent interest in the so-called 'banana wars' at the WTO, partly because the allies invited as many key players as possible, with funding for Southern allies who could not otherwise have travelled to Brussels.

By the time of the second conference, the South–South–North alliance had managed to mobilise a number of food retail companies that had emerged as the lead firms in the banana economy (and most other sectors of grocery), accounting for the lion's share of profits along the chain. Multinational companies like Tesco and Walmart, but also big national retailers like J. Sainsbury in the UK, Coop and Migros in Switzerland or Coop Italia in Italy that had developed enormous purchasing power in relation to their suppliers came to the table, more or less willingly. The banana split graphics produced by BL had become familiar exhibits in corporate boardrooms, increasingly embarrassed by the disproportionately large contribution that the margins from sales of one product made to the annual profit sheet.[6]

At this stage, the large-scale retail companies were just beginning the process of responding to emerging pressures from their own national civil societies over the negative social and environmental impacts in the product chains from which these 'gatekeepers' to consumers sourced what they sold in their stores. Without pressure – real and perceived – from 'customers', usually articulated by civil society organisations, although rarely consumer organisations per se, the supermarket chains would not have started to design strategies to face up to the critiques coming at them over the hidden costs of some of their key product lines (for instance, imported fresh produce, clothing, meat, fish/seafood, palm oil).

The major multiple retailers, largely supplied at the time by major multinational banana brands – Chiquita, Del Monte, Dole and Fyffes – had become 'price setters' rather than 'price takers'. German discount retailer Aldi had even come to set an unofficial EU banana price to which other retailers referred in their own buying contracts with the multinational brands or the newly emerging national plantation-owning companies like Acon in Costa Rica, Reybanpac/Wong in Ecuador or Agroamérica in Guatemala. The 'Aldi price' for an imported banana box became the weekly reference, but this price was under growing downward pressure as competition from other retailers – well beyond Europe's biggest market in Germany – came to define the economic behaviour of grocers across the EU27 over the following years.

Confronting retailers with challenging messages

Banana Link had begun to seek to influence these retailers following its participation in a 1996 campaign led by British NGO Christian Aid that focused public attention on the violations of basic labour rights in international food supply chains. The success of this consumer awareness and action campaign had led to the creation in 1998 of the tripartite ETI by the major retail brands also targeted by a public campaign (Christian Aid, 2007), in collaboration with British and international trade unions and the biggest UK development NGOs. The ETI garnered the support of the UK's Department for International Development who remained its main funder for 20 years.

Engagement by organised labour with this kind of multi-stakeholder process since the origins of ETI has broadened the vision and strategic visions of unions that have traditionally focused on industrial relations between their direct employers and their members. A critical mass of leaders have developed the skills required to seek transparency, establish dialogue and, ultimately, convince lead firms – in this case major retailers – to accept their responsibilities as corporate citizens and adapt their sourcing strategies.

In 1999, a BL postcard campaign targeting Tesco and Asda/Walmart[7] as members of the newly founded ETI focused on violations of trade union rights and, for the first time, on the environmental and health impacts of excessive agrochemical use in the retailers' Costa Rican supplier plantations, with all the information supplied by plantation-based labour unions. BL's key role in response to their request was to remind lead firms of their written commitment to the ETI Base Code on Labour Standards to ensuring a 'living wage' (ETI clause), to facilitate the space to open dialogue around a broad range of specific issues, and be at the table to advocate workers' concerns when a multi-stakeholder player like ETI facilitated such a space.

In 2003, BL contributed key information gleaned over many years from UK importers on the distribution of value along the retailers' supply chains to a seminal study by the NGO platform UK Food Group (2003) entitled *Food Inc: Corporate Concentration from Farm to Consumer*. This report laid out for the first time in detail the role of globalised supermarket buyers in squeezing prices paid to growers and thereby forcing – or maintaining – low workers' wages (labour accounting for 30 to 60 per cent of banana production costs).

A key moment in the rise of power of the new lead firms was the retail price war on bananas in the UK, initiated in 2002 by Asda/Walmart on the back of an exclusive low-price deal with Fresh Del Monte. This move signalled the start of one of the most significant value-stripping processes in recent commodity history: over the following decade, retailers abandoned the lucrative margins that had prevailed in Europe's second biggest banana market. The Walmart-inspired move drove a race to the bottom in prices to consumers that in turn accelerated a race to the bottom in working and contractual conditions for plantation workers and pushed investment in the sector to the lowest cost and least stringent regulatory environments in the producer countries of the Global South.

A permanent multi-stakeholder forum is born

Following the second international conference, the alliance decided to move into proactive mode in the absence of any space in which the common South–South–North agenda we had designed could be discussed with other players on a regular basis. We proposed to members of FAO's Inter-Governmental Group on Bananas and Tropical Fruit the creation of a permanent multi-stakeholder forum (Second International Banana Conference, 2005, 2006). BL organised a series of consultations and advocacy events with governments – hosted by the UN Conference on Trade and Development (UNCTAD) – on our trade policy proposals, as well as with fruit and retail companies at Dutch trade union confederation FNV headquarters. Throughout this process, EUROBAN continued to provide the strategic space in which the civil society alliance met to analyse developments with the different industry stakeholders and plan our responses and activities.

Chiquita was the first banana company prepared to publicly accompany BL and EUROBAN in promoting the creation of a permanent forum on achieving sustainable production and trade, later to be joined by Dole following an international campaign focusing on labour rights in their plantations (Feral et al, 2006). So, when the FAO Trade and Markets Division approached BL and our allies to help establish a formal preparatory process to launch what became the World Banana Forum (WBF), our job of convincing the three leading global retailers – then Walmart, Carrefour and Tesco – to participate in a series of Preparatory Committee meetings was made much easier by the knowledge that the two biggest banana brands were supportive. FAO was able to mobilise several member governments to join UNCTAD and the ILO on the governmental and inter-governmental side of the tripartite committee charged with launching the permanent multi-stakeholder forum.

Two of the critical differences with other such fora or so-called 'round tables' set up in the 2000s are first that the WBF was co-founded with governments of banana-exporting countries that play a role in the ongoing work and second that it has, since its creation, ensured that the economic dimensions of production and trade – especially the links between the distribution of value and decent work on the one hand, and fair prices and margins on the other – are given as much transparent attention as the social and environmental dimensions of sustainability. Other sectoral initiatives tend to exclude any discussion on wages, social benefits, prices, costs of sustainable production and externalities.

The banana sector, under the influence of a strong and coordinated workers', farmers' and critical consumers' agenda, has positioned these issues at the heart of a process designed to transform a highly unsustainable industry into one that provides decent livelihoods, safe work and healthy products with no costs to current and future generations. Despite their historically weak voice and bargaining power, organised workers and family farmers have used the leverage of the lead firms' biggest food line not only to secure a place at the table, but to help set the agenda discussed there.

When the WBF was launched in 2009 in Rome, multinational retailers Tesco and Walmart were protagonists in the lively debates that included, crucially, these sensitive economic issues around wages, prices and the distribution of value. The lead firm chairing the session on the distribution of value even initiated the debate by suggesting, albeit a touch provocatively: 'why don't we just agree to set a global minimum fair banana price?'

Navigating complexity as a prerequisite for influencing lead firms

A critical part of the mutual learning between the organisations at the beginning of the chains and those at the consumer end has been the building of critical knowledge and understanding of lead firm 'sourcing' strategies and the business context in which they make decisions affecting the lives of hundreds of millions. These strategies are part of the complex web of issues that organised workers and family farmers are currently seeking to influence, conscious that our messages about an unfair distribution of value have on occasions reached big retail boardrooms.

The economic power of the lead firms to determine the terms of trade and therefore the framework in which negotiations back down the chain take place is a social construction at one level, rather than a 'given' that is too hard to challenge. The shifting ground at the beginning of the third decade of the 21st century is calling many such assumptions into question, including those to do with seemingly structural inequalities and radical imbalances of power.

The strategic response of big retail to the shifting ground of the last two decades is in this sense a fertile source of learning as to how organised 'weak' voices can start to influence more and more directly the strategies of global businesses and the values with which they operate. The emergence of legal requirements to social and environmental reporting, of binding HRDD legislation initiatives actively supported by some big retailers, the post-COVID-19 drive to bring together and address concerns over human rights at work and environmental sustainability management strands inside management systems in some of the lead firms, as well as to source deliberately from smaller family farmer organisations, are all significant indicators that workers and small farmer voices are being heard more and more clearly at senior management level of firms. While the emergence – in the framework of increasingly tangible climatic deregulation and a global zoonosis-induced pandemic – of a questioning of the very modes of production, such as disease-prone industrial monoculture in the case of bananas, opens the field for even more interesting innovations and value system changes.

A timely reminder that a 'race to the top' between lead firms is a pragmatic utopia worth aiming for comes from Oxfam International's *Behind the Barcodes* campaign launched in 2018, with input from the South–South–North civil society banana alliance. Sixteen lead firms are being tracked by the NGO and ranked in an annual 'Supermarket Scorecard' designed to encourage the retailers to ameliorate their impacts in four domains: transparency, labour rights, small farmer sourcing and women.

Innovative proposals from the ground up

Small farmers' organisations that are still involved in the global trade, partly thanks to the opportunity provided by Fairtrade certification and therefore minimum prices well above conventional market prices, are breaking out of the monoculture model that even the best voluntary certification systems have tended to encourage. They have started exploring the possibility to sell directly to the lead firms, through their own farmer-controlled exporting companies, while continuing to transform livelihoods and diversify their production systems agroecologically, financed by the higher prices commanded by organic fairly traded bananas. BL is requested to help them present the case that fresh and processed produce from biodiverse systems could and should become a new selling point to increasingly conscious consumers.

Attempts since the early 2000s by trade unions to promote 'unionised bananas' in Northern Europe were frustrated by fellow industry players who regarded the short-lived experiment in Norway, for example, as the 'threat of a good example'. A few years on, although the idea of a trade union label never came to fruition, not least because the proliferation of labels and claims had already crowded out the marketplace, there are signals from some of the big German or British retailers that their firms might be prepared to purchase directly from family farmer-controlled exporters. In 2020, the first moves by big retail to shift sourcing from non-union workplaces to unionised ones are also potentially game-changing. Recent developments in the WBF to validate the role of labour unions in negotiating living wages for all plantation and packhouse workers is another important result of the South-based organisations' active engagement in convincing retailers that decent work and a fairer distribution of value is where consumer awareness is driving the lead firms.

Looking ahead, the first conversations between organised workers and lead firms about trade unions taking on a direct role in the verification of compliance with decent standards are starting to take place. Given the importance that lead firms have given to arms-length private certification processes, over the last two decades, this engagement and the questions it raises about the proactive role of workers at the beginning of long international production chains are also very significant.

Putting gender equity at the heart of common action to transform the sector

Another area of dialogue with the lead firms which is gaining ground fast is in the cross-cutting area of gender equity. Over 25 years of work by Latin American women packhouse workers within their own unions, at regional level in COLSIBA, and since 2015 within the WBF is shifting the boundaries of discussion and now practice by lead firms, both in terms of non-discrimination, but also in terms of women's employment and empowerment both within plantation workplaces and in the companies along the chain.

Women's empowerment, at all levels of the industry, started with Honduran women working in Chiquita packhouses in the mid-1990s (Frank, 2005). Their journey started by raising their own awareness of their rights and how to exercise them, then progressed to feminising plantation trade union leadership in their own country and across the continent through COLSIBA, advocating workplace improvements using a common platform of demands developed by women workers across Central and South America, sharing collective bargaining practices and clauses, challenging the companies that employ them to aim for zero sexual harassment and gender-based violence, raising the awareness of male colleagues, accepting the challenges of the triple burden when taking leadership positions, often as the single head of a household.

In the last few years, this journey has begun to reach the eyes, ears and consciences of lead firm managers, often women themselves, but not always. Recent developments at UK-based Tesco (2020) demonstrate that it is possible for a lead firm to produce a serious global gender strategy across all agri-food chains supplying the company, based in particular on women's experiences in the banana sector where they are a small majority – as low as 7 per cent of the total workforce in some countries (Cooper, 2015), and with resources allocated for rolling this strategy out. The role of BL and COLSIBA in developing this strategy has been directly acknowledged by the company.

In 2020, several years of unfruitful dialogue over labour and trade union rights with one of the leading global fruit brands reached a turning point when the company gave senior women managers the mandate to take the dialogue in hand and steer conflicts towards resolution. Meanwhile, one of its largest customers, a lead firm in retail in the Americas, the UK and Asia, is exploring the possibility of women's empowerment training in an environment where hostility from the producing companies to any level of cooperation with trade unions is notorious, in the hope that this can provide a lever for change, for installing good faith dialogue and ultimately enshrining improvements through the route of bargaining for collective contracts.

Finally, leading producers in Africa and South America are now exploring how far they can go to remove obstacles to women's employment, to what extent the evident positive socioeconomic development externalities of employing more women can be taken into account, especially when it comes to many of the field tasks. What do 'women-friendly' workplaces actually look like and how to invest the necessary resources in an environment where prices paid to producers barely cover costs of production, let alone sustainable production based on genuinely decent work for women and men? What difference does employing more women managers make to the company's economic performance?

When fruit companies start asking such questions and are prepared to accept the sometimes uncomfortable answers, it is not unreasonable to imagine a world where lead firms themselves could even lead a 'race to the top', raising the bar for all, starting with the most vulnerable and marginalised people employed in their hitherto de-humanised supply chains.

Conclusion

If BL were to try to schematise the modes that our team has used over the past 25 years to influence lead firms in support of a transformative agenda proposed by our workers' and farmers' organisation partners in the banana producing and exporting countries of the Global South, Table 7.2 is offered as a summary of how our *modus operandi* has evolved over time.

In the first years of BL's life as an organisation the emphasis was on gathering and relaying information from sources on the ground, usually from the same partners in banana exporting territories with which we still work. When retailers first engaged with civil society as a result of public campaigns highlighting the responsibility they needed to accept, it was through the newly appointed ethical trade or

Table 7.2: Evolution of civil society's role in influencing the lead firm to change

Awareness of territorial impacts in producing countries	Engaging with ethical, commercial and technical managers	Co-constructing an agenda and activities to ameliorate negative impacts	Engaging in multi-stakeholder processes to transform the global industry

CSR managers of the lead firms recruited to represent them in the first phase of dialogue and company responses. As our knowledge of the chains increased, along with our capacity and credibility for dialogue, wherever possible with a partner in the room, so we were able to move to the co-construction of the agenda with lead firm managers, including those with commercial and technical responsibilities. At the same time, and with increasing intensity and scope, especially once the WBF and the permanent working groups started to function fully, the conversations, actions and reactions have started to open up to reflection – and potentially to action – that could see global retail's biggest selling food product pioneering transformative pathways of significance well beyond the world of perishable fruit.

Notes

[1] Reference to the 'slave triangle', a triangular trading system that operated from the late 16th century to early 19th century, carrying slaves, cash crops, and manufactured goods between West Africa, Caribbean or American colonies and within the northern colonies of British North America. See for instance: https://slavetrianglex.weebly.com/what-is-the-slave-triangle.html.

[2] As indicated on the Facebook page of the association, www.facebook.com/WindwardIslandsFarmersAssociation/

[3] Registered as a not-for-profit cooperative company limited by guarantee in January 1996.

[4] For example, a postcard campaign requesting support from the European Commission and EU member state governments for an EU fair trade banana quota mobilised 150,000 individual postcards in six countries.

[5] See www.iuf.org for the full name of the organisation and its membership.

[6] One lead firm CEO was even photographed for the media in front of an in-store banana display, where he had gone to announce record profits. Our own estimates in the early 2000s were that fresh bananas contributed up to 2 per cent of all historic profits to UK retailers (who sell tens of thousands of lines).

[7] US-based international retailer Walmart bought the UK's second biggest retail chain in 1999. Walmart pulled out of Germany in 2006, leaving the UK as its only direct presence on European soil.

References

Banana Link (2020) Objectives, vision and priorities, www.bananalink.org.uk/about/our-objectives/

BASIC (2015) *Banana Value Chains in Europe and the Consequences of Unfair Trading Practices*, www.bananalink.org.uk/wp-content/uploads/2019/04/banana_value_chain_research_FINAL_WEB.pdf

Christian Aid (2007) *No Small Change: Christian Aid's Understanding of How Change Happens*, www.christianaid.org.uk/sites/default/files/2017-08/no-small-change-december-2007-updated-2010.pdf

Cooper, A. (2015) *Women in the Banana Export Industry: Global Overview*, Banana Link, www.bananalink.org.uk/wp-content/uploads/2019/04/FINAL-ENG_Global-Overview_FAO-Gender-research-2015.pdf

Feral, M., Fischer, H., Nielsen, J. and Smith, A. (2006) *Dole, Behind the Smokescreen* ... Peuples Solidaires, Banana Link, CTM, COSIBA-CR, FENACLE, UNTRAFLORES, Alan Irvine and Florian Coat, www.iufdocuments.org/www/documents/DoleReport-e.pdf

Frank, D. (2005) *Bananeras: Women Transforming the Banana Unions of Latin America*, South End Press.

Second International Banana Conference (2005) *Final Report*, www.fao.org/fileadmin/templates/banana/documents/IBC2_finalReport_en05.pdf

Second International Banana Conference (2006) *Towards a Multi-Stakeholder Forum on Bananas*, www.fao.org/fileadmin/templates/banana/documents/IBC2_TowardsAmultistakeholderForumOnBananas_en06.pdf

Smith, A. (2010) *La Saga de la Banane*, Editions Charles Léopold Mayer.

Tesco Stores plc (2020) *Gender – Supply Chain Strategy*, www.tescoplc.com/sustainability/publications/policies/downloads/gender-supply-chain-strategy/

Thomson, R. (1987) *Green Gold: Bananas and Dependency in the Eastern Caribbean*, Latin America Bureau.

UK Food Group (2003) *Food Inc.: Corporate Concentration from Farm to Consumer*, www.researchgate.net/publication/270285330_Food_Inc_Corporate_Concentration_from_Farm_to_Consumer/link/54a6ed470cf257a6360ab147/download

EIGHT

Empowering local communities in their struggle for land and rights

Eloïse Maulet

This chapter recounts the organising strategy developed by the French-based civil society initiative ReAct through the unfolding of a campaign led against the abuses by Socfin and Bolloré in and around their rubber and oil palm plantations. Land occupied, a lack of living space, rivers polluted, forests destroyed, a sacred place and indigenous cemeteries wiped out: the oil palm and rubber agro-industrial activities of Socfin Group have affected local communities for many decades. Yet, most of these issues are still unresolved or have not given rise to fair compensation. For almost ten years, the association ReAct has supported the local communities' struggle against human rights violations and environmental destruction, in order to tackle corporate impunity step by step. ReAct's strategy has involved:

- strengthening grassroots power;
- connecting people and building a transnational alliance; and

- identifying leverage points and running campaigns at a global level.

Local communities organised at a local and global level have worked together to achieve important victories in this David versus Goliath fight, even if the challenges in the years ahead remain significant.

Palm oil and rubber: value unfairly distributed along the product chains

Oil palm and rubber monocultures can have significant negative impacts on local communities and the environment. These adverse effects are sometimes very poorly compensated despite the fact that the company generates significant profits. The Socfin Group was created in 1909. Specialising in the development and management of agro-industrial plantations, it operates in ten African and Asian countries where it has 15 industrial-scale palm and rubber tree plantations. The Group's different subsidiaries run various activities ranging from plantation management to marketing and scientific research. Its holdings and operating companies in Europe are based in Belgium, Switzerland, France and Luxembourg.[1] The Group's main shareholder is the Belgian businessman Hubert Fabri with a 54 per cent stake[2] followed by the Bolloré Group with 39.4 per cent.[3] Socfin's profits (EBITDA) for 2019 amounted to €152 million. Between 2009 and 2018, the Group's planted area increased from 129,658 to 194,000 hectares[4] (+49.6 per cent). This sharp ten-year growth in areas occupied by monocultures has heightened tensions with local communities over land issues, and conflicts were exacerbated by a lack of transparency regarding plantation boundaries, inefficient retrocessions of land, and expansion into wetlands.

The Socfin Group holds 387,939 hectares of concessions for its plantations. This affects 42 villages in Cameroon, 13 villages in Côte d'Ivoire, seven villages (850 families) in Cambodia, 52 villages in Sierra Leone and 81 villages in Liberia: a total of nearly 200 villages with thousands of people impacted in these five countries alone. The people who formerly occupied this land earned their livelihood mainly from growing food crops and using natural resources from forests and rivers. As a result, they have been deprived of most of their means of survival. In some cases, the villagers agreed to give up their land to the plantations in exchange for promises of jobs and development made some ten years ago by Socfin Group. However, in the long run, the infrastructure and jobs that actually materialised have failed to make up for the loss of their land. The local community representatives denounced these unkept promises, especially the obligations contracted under the sales agreement with Socfin, namely the continuity of the public service mission (education, healthcare, housing), road maintenance, and so on. Moreover, according to Socfin's own figures, 19,368 of its plantation workers are precarious workers.[5] As Guillaume Nyobe, a resident of Koungue Somse in Cameroon underlines, 'the only jobs offered to local residents are those of casual worker, labourer and tractor driver'.

The establishment of these plantations and their subsequent expansion have caused substantial deforestation, thus depleting a resource that is crucial for the local and indigenous communities, such as the Pygmies in Cameroon or the Bunong in Cambodia. In Cameroon, Liberia, Sierra Leone, Côte d'Ivoire and Cambodia, hundreds of people had their access to drinking water impaired due to the activities of Socfin plantations. In Cameroon, for example, at the Mbongo, Eseka and Kienké plantations, the lagoons used by the palm oil mills to treat their wastewater were clearly dysfunctional as the wastewater flowed directly into nearby rivers used by residents. This was also the case for wastewater from the SoGB rubber factory in Côte d'Ivoire, which emptied into a nearby backwater. In the vicinity of the Safacam plantation in Cameroon, in the Dizangue district, community members reported having witnessed the disappearance of three water sources. In Cambodia, Bunong farmers were concerned about growing health problems (stomach ache, in particular) which they believed were water-related. In their view, the chemicals such as herbicides and fertilisers used on the plantations went directly into their water sources. The same is true in Liberia, where many inhabitants from villages near the plantations and who used the chemically polluted water complained of stomach ache and diarrhoea.

In Sierra Leone's Malen Chiefdom, the impact of the use of chemicals, fertilisers, pesticides and herbicides was also criticised by local communities. In 2013, chemical pollution of the Malen River was confirmed by the national Environment Protection Agency in response to a complaint made by the communities following reports of large numbers of dead fish. In addition to deforestation and water pollution, neighbouring local communities were concerned about air pollution from particles (SO_2, Nox, CO) emitted by rubber processing plants and palm oil mills. They had no access to comprehensive data guaranteeing them that these activities pose no health risk for those who breathe the air in the vicinity of the plants. For the most part, environmental impact studies are scarce and difficult to access. In conflict situations, or in contexts permitting the abuse of power, women are particularly vulnerable. Women from villages near the plantations in Sierra Leone, Cameroon and Liberia have testified to numerous cases of assault and violence, whether they work on the plantation or not. Many women who have to cross the plantation to reach their own fields or produce their own artisanal palm oil are threatened and some have been physically harmed. "If you're unlucky, you only get your salary if you let the supervisor do his thing," explains a woman who works as a daily worker on the SRC plantation in Liberia.

In the face of powerlessness and isolation, collective organisation

Given the deprivation of resources, the lack of job opportunities, environmental damages and insecurity, the communities became increasingly aware that they were victims of injustice. To cope with the anger triggered by this feeling of injustice and to change the status quo, the locals resorted to different kinds of actions throughout the conflict. Yet, these often lead to two different kinds of impasse.

The impasse created by illusions

One strategy is to call on the benevolence and goodwill of the other party in the conflict. It involves appealing to the other party's willingness to sacrifice some of their interests for the wellbeing of those impacted by their activities. However, the adversary's economic rationale and administrative constraints often make it unresponsive to the language of charity and morals. This method is frequently advocated by some traditional headmen. It generates a long list of letters and meetings with plantation management or with government representatives, but these never achieve any tangible outcome except vague promises and a token monetary remuneration for the meeting attendees. In the district of Kienké, Cameroon, the traditional headman showed the 18 letters he had written to the plantation's general manager and the prefect of the region requesting meetings. He also showed the letters written by the Mabi Headmen's association, comprising seven headmen of villages near the plantation. Most of these letters remained unanswered and nothing significant has ever come of the few meetings that took place as a result. Moreover, such meetings were looked on with distaste by locals, who saw them as a sign that the headmen had been bought off by Socfin's subsidiary, Socapalm. When the balance of power is so unequal, appealing to the decision makers is tantamount to begging, which is unlikely to result in a conflict resolution that is satisfactory for both parties.

The impasse created by blind anger

Driven by the failure of the first strategy, the exasperation and fatigue of the dominated most often find expression in sporadic eruptions of violence, for instance in the form of riots. This path often results in an impasse due not only to the strategic weakness of the blows received, but most of all to a lack of awareness of negotiating logic. The absence of a reliable representative or spokesperson, the sporadic nature of protests and the effectiveness of repressive measures are some of the many factors that lead the adversary to not prioritise the avenue of negotiation. On almost every plantation, we observed regular cases of the population rising up against the company: in November 2010 in Kienké, Cameroon, Socapalm employees who had come to take measurements for the plantation's extension were attacked by residents with machetes; a bulldozer and its driver were shot by arrows in Bikondo on the same plantation; a bulldozer was burnt in Bu Sra, Cambodia in 2008; in Cameroon, the residents attacked Socfin company offices, vandalising and burning company houses, after residents had been abused by the security firm, Africa Security; in Liberia in 2007, Socfin employees were attacked with machetes during the burning of villages for the expansion of the Liberian Agricultural Company (LAC).

In most cases, the intervention of law enforcement officials eventually brought the situation under control. Sometimes, these incidents were followed by a visit from the local authorities (with or without the plantation director) to listen to the local communities' grievances and, sometimes, the company promised to maintain 'neighbourly relations'. Yet, most often, these initiatives for dialogue in the wake of local uprisings quickly petered out once stability had been restored. To help find a way out of these impasses, in some countries ReAct supported the local communities affected by Socfin's activities by introducing methods to help the communities self-organise so that they could climb the four steps to empowerment:

- Organise collectively
- Express concrete demands
- Take non-violent action
- Negotiate

The four-step staircase tool (Figure 8.1) was developed over the process of the Bolloré/Socfin campaign to offer a third path as a method of conflict resolution in an asymmetrical socioeconomic conflict. Building on the activists' ongoing experience and diverse analytical sources which inspired our work, it aims to compensate for the limits of the impasse situations. The impasses hold two key messages: 'No negotiation without power', and 'No action without the prospect of negotiation'. The tool describes a process enabling a reconciliation of the parties' interests in order to ease conflict. Developed in a specific context, the tool can be used in all conflict situations in which a dominant, homogeneous actor opposes a disorganised group of people whose interests are being trampled. The staircase concept relies on two main theoretical foundations: the theory of negotiation and the sociology of collective action. Under what circumstances could negotiation lead to a fair compromise in a situation of asymmetrical power?

The feeling of injustice as a cement for the foundations of the process

The first element of conflict, in its most basic form, that this process seeks to transform is individual anger. This is sometimes described as a feeling of frustration or deprivation born from the perceived gap between the good which people feel entitled to – value expectations – and the good which they think they can obtain – value capabilities (Gurr, 1970). This anger can sometimes be expressed as a feeling of injustice whereby one

Figure 8.1: The four-step staircase

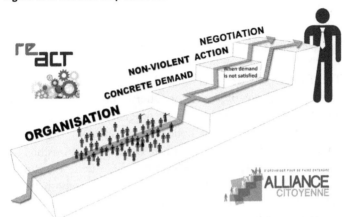

Source: ReAct and Alliance Citoyenne

considers oneself a victim (Gamson et al, 1982). The term 'anger' is used to translate these sociological concepts into simple language. It involves recognising that anger is a positive emotion and that we are right to be angry in unjust situations. In the case studied, the feeling of injustice and the anger of local communities affected by Socfin's activities came from:

- *non-compliance with standards and commitments:* sometimes contractual/written promises had raised expectations regarding compensation, jobs, or social infrastructure for instance, but had not been fulfilled;
- *the communities' realisation that treatment was unequal:* for example, the situation in some areas of Cameroon worsened when the plantations were privatised or cultivated areas were expanded. This made people aware of the gap between 'before' and 'now'. They were also able to compare the situation in other plantations either run by other companies or located in other countries, which highlighted a gap between 'elsewhere' and 'here'.

Given this 'shared anger', the first step in the staircase is to work on collective organisation.

The path to collective organisation

This first step draws on classical theories of collective action, particularly those of Anthony Oberschall (1973), who sets out the necessary conditions for progressing to action. The minimum conditions for collective organisation are shared objectives and the identification of those responsible for the injustices perpetrated. However, these basic conditions will only lead to weak forms of protest. To establish robust collective action that can be repeated, Oberschall identifies two structural factors: an organisational base and a continuity of the established movement. For each of these two factors, Oberschall highlights the need to use existing resources, such as villages, families and communities. Traditional community solidarity is an important resource for structuring strong collective organisations that produce recognised leaders and goals. For Oberschall, weak organisational capacity is the main cause of short-lived, violent and ill-thought-out revolts, such as the peasant revolts described by historian George Rudé, which occurred in France before the 1789 Revolution, or even the contemporary urban riots in the American ghettos and French suburbs.

In early 2010, thanks to different online platforms and websites actively monitoring corporate-generated social conflicts and abuses by multinational companies, the founding members of ReAct identified conflicts between Socfin and the communities living on Socfin plantations in Cameroon through several research projects and testimonies. For example, Bolloré Group, one of the Group's shareholders, was suing Radio France Inter reporter Benoit Collombat for defamation on account of his report 'Cameroon, the Black Empire of Vincent Bolloré'. During the trial, David N., a resident in one of the affected villages in the Kienké region, who had been living in France for several years, came to testify on behalf of the journalist. Brandishing a storm lamp, he tried to describe the difficult conditions in which the local communities were still living, without electricity, while at the same time the company's power supply line was just nearby. This event led to initial contacts between ReAct members and the people directly concerned, first, in several villages bordering the Socapalm Kienké plantation in the south of the country, then around the Dimbombari plantation, west of Douala. From village to village, the same anger was expressed, the same issues described and listed.

ReAct then engaged with the local communities in their struggle to defend their rights. ReAct's goal was to help the people impacted by this multinational find a way out of the impasses, starting with first step of the four-step staircase tool. The association supported the collective organisation of these villages, first, by helping to link up people from affected villages located around a given plantation. For example, the Kienké plantation in Cameroon is surrounded by 11 villages, the SoGB plantation in Côte d'Ivoire by 13 villages that claim to have been displaced, and the LAC in Liberia by more than 20 villages. Next, linkages were established between different plantations within the same country – Sofcin owns seven oil palm and rubber plantations in Cameroon, two in Liberia – and, finally, between plantations in different countries – Socfin is present in ten countries in Africa and Asia.

An initial information-sharing effort helped to better identify the shared feelings of anger and injustice uniting the villages. The first meetings were organised between village leaders of the Dimbobari and Kienké plantations in Cameroon, where the people present were able to tell their stories and identify shared interests. Later on, the residents of villages in Cameroon, Côte d'Ivoire and Liberia shared photos and videos, as well as documents such as letters sent, local agreements, or newspaper articles. Information on the Socfin and Bolloré Groups in the form of activity reports, key figures or press releases was transmitted locally and analysed.

Gradually, the different elements of collective organisation were set up and strengthened in the different countries – first in Cameroon, then in Côte d'Ivoire, Liberia, Cambodia and Sierra Leone. Local communities around some of the plantations were already trying to organise themselves into associations, despite local repressive actions. This was the case in Sierra Leone with the Malen Affected Land Owners and Land Users Association (MALOA). ReAct was thus able to support the collective dynamic by deploying methodological tools. Elsewhere, organisations were built from scratch by bringing together the first leaders and forming a collective, as in Cameroon with the Dynari association – later to become Synaparcam. In some regions, those directly concerned were trying to organise collectively but faced challenges from non-democratic and non-representative organisations that were sometimes backed by the company to ensure that any opposition was not too disruptive. In these circumstances, setting up new democratic membership organisations often proved more difficult than in cases where there was no pre-existing organisation. The company's local managers, at times supported by the local authorities, were applying the 'divide and rule' strategy by delegitimising the actors involved, slowing down administrative procedures, or repressing and arresting key community leaders.

During the second step – after the first step of networking and organising collectively – the local communities worked on formulating their demands, mainly during their local assemblies. Village by village, they identified the problems caused by the Socfin plantation's operations – problems that had persisted or were even worsening. To produce concrete demands, they mainly drew on the oral or written promises that had been made by the company in the past. For example, in Liberia, senior management at the LAC plantation had signed an agreement in 2007 with the local community delegates and government representatives, listing the company's responsibilities regarding housing, water and sanitation, new educational and health facilities and so on. In Cameroon, a sales agreement framing the privatisation of the Socapalm plantation in 2000 defined the purchaser's obligations notably with respect to the continuation of the public service mission in the fields of health, education or housing. On the basis of clearly listed problems linked to the activities of the Socfin plantations, they drew up their demands together with proposed solutions. Thereafter, the communities arranged the demands in order of priority so as to build a campaign strategy. As will be seen later, thanks to the collective organisation, the demands were structured on a local scale, first for the villages, then shared more widely to scale up from the local to global level.

Developing a repertoire of actions

The third step in the staircase model is inspired by the sociology of social movements and derived from the 'social-movement repertoire' developed by Charles Tilly. In fact, this step requires that the actors use the organisational foundations put in place to develop a repertoire of possible actions. It involves drawing on knowledge of the field, mobilising symbols that resonate with people's lives and incentivise their mobilisation, and possibly promoting visibility to the outside world via the media. Although this notion of a social-movement repertoire is different from that used by Tilly, who attempted to trace it over the long-term history of European social movements, or from the work of Gene Sharp, who researched and catalogued 198 methods of non-violent action (Sharp, 1973), it allowed us to put together a toolbox of actions that could be used as leverage during negotiations. The diversity and variable impacts of actions from the repertoire will strengthen the position of the people involved in negotiations by multiplying the possible BATNAs (Best Alternative To Negotiated Agreement) at each stage. It is important to identify the actions that can be mobilised in conjunction with a negotiation process.

Those affected need to develop their capacity to act in order to limit the concentrations of power that can lead to violations of human and environmental rights. Non-violent direct action is thus at the centre of the approach. Non-violent direct action is action by people, for themselves, against those whose interests oppose their emancipation. It places the individual in a position of being active. 'It is a remedy against the feeling of powerlessness. It teaches self-confidence. To act oneself!' (Pouget, 2008 [1904]: 2) It is also valuable as a form of civic and political education. Direct action is the power of those who have nothing but their capacity to act. Direct action makes it possible to avoid the first impasse created by illusions, while non-violence enables the second impasse to be avoided and helps to open up a negotiating and conflict resolution process.

We are not alone: building a transnational alliance

The local communities affected, with support from ReAct, ensured coordination between different countries – initially, to share information and compare situations, then to join forces and build common demands and, finally, to carry out synchronised collective actions. On 5 June 2013, the local organisations of the communities neighbouring the Socfin and Bolloré Group plantations in five countries (Liberia, Sierra Leone, Cameroon, Cambodia and Côte d'Ivoire), expressed their common demands in a letter addressed to the Bolloré Group CEO. To deliver it to Vincent Bolloré, they decided to organise a global day of action on the day that the Group's annual shareholder meeting was to be held in Paris. The communities all took action simultaneously in each of their countries. In Sierra Leone, several hundred villagers occupied the land of the SAC plantation. In Côte d'Ivoire, a peaceful march of residents was blocked by police forces as they approached the main factory and the administrative offices to deliver their message to the management of the SoGB plantation. In Douala, Cameroon, 200 farm workers and traditional leaders walked to the Socapalm plantation headquarters in their traditional mourning dress to symbolise the loss they were suffering. In Paris, people from Cameroon, Côte d'Ivoire and other affected countries occupied the Bolloré Group's headquarters. They carried watering cans, hand shovels and rakes, and set about tending the lawn outside the headquarters. "We don't have any more land in our country, so we have to plant cassava in your yard!" exclaimed a man from a village in Cameroon who was directly affected by the plantation's activities. This first synchronised action embodied the creation of the Transnational Alliance of Local Communities Affected by Socfin Bolloré Plantations, and was the final scale-up from local to international level.

In response to ongoing pressure from the Alliance's members, Bolloré agreed to meet with representatives from the villagers' organisations. The first transnational negotiation took place in Paris on 24 October 2014. The Bolloré Group agreed to an independent land assessment that would shed light on the land conflicts, and to a meeting the following year in order to track the progress made. It was also specifically agreed that Socfin representatives would attend the follow-up meeting as they had ignored the Alliance's request that they appear at the first meeting. However, the negotiation timeline was not respected as Bolloré did not involve Socfin in the dialogue and Socfin continued to refuse to take part. This first encouraging opening of the dialogue thus came to a halt. Thereafter, the Socfin and Bolloré Groups handed over negotiating responsibility to local management and attempted to publicise the few positive steps taken. However, these were far from meeting the demands of local residents affected by their operations.

Relocating the fight

Faced with the refusal of decision makers to negotiate at the international level, the communities were compelled to step up local momentum. This sparked a new series of actions between April and June 2015: peaceful protests in the plantations of Djbombari and Mbongo in Cameroon, a march to the LAC plantation management offices in Liberia, a sit-in in Cambodia, and a large people's assembly in Côte d'Ivoire. These actions led to renewed local negotiations in Cameroon, Liberia, and Cambodia. Tripartite platforms were set up for negotiations to take place in Cameroon and Cambodia between the company, the local authorities and the communities. The same year, several transnational solidarity actions were organised to protest against the arrest of organisation leaders in Liberia and Sierra Leone, which resulted in their release. However, the charges against some leaders were maintained as a pressure and other criminal lawsuits were later filed by Socfin in Sierra Leone.

Strengthening grassroots power: community organisation in remote areas

Given the stance of the Socfin and Bolloré Groups, which both refused to manage the conflict at international level, the local dimension had to be strengthened. To facilitate the mobilisations in the different countries and different plantations, the local organisations were compelled to organise and structure themselves more effectively.

After the first phase of supporting collective organisation by linking up those directly affected had successfully led to the creation of the Transnational Alliance of Local Communities Affected by Socfin Bolloré Plantations, ReAct then focused on helping to strengthen several local organisations. Given the lengthy struggle for their rights and the multinational's power, the local communities were obliged to organise themselves more sustainably and develop a long-term strategy. Drawing on community-organising methods developed by Saul Alinsky (1971) and on the model designed by the Association of Community Organizations for Reform Now (ACORN), ReAct worked to strengthen the tools, methods and skills required for effective local community organisation. This enabled ReAct to provide more robust support to local organisations, particularly in Cameroon and Liberia. Alinsky (1971) adapted the tactics for trade union organisation, action and negotiation in a factory environment to apply them to defending citizens' rights. Moreover, he formalised the organisational function by making the mission of recruitment and organisation-building into a real profession. The ACORN community-organising model defines in detail the role of an organiser and sets out the different steps for constructing a community organisation: 'the organising drive'. Strategic and tactical elements are also described in detail to enable members of an organisation to conduct campaigns. ReAct's community organisers thus provided support for organising the residents of the villages surrounding the plantations. According to this approach, there are five ingredients for effective organisation:

- *A group of people who coordinate themselves*: a vast number of people became members of the supported organisation, thanks to recruitment efforts by the organisers, particularly in Liberia and Cameroon.
- *A collective identity*: this was built on a shared feeling of injustice, with each organisation having a name specific to each country, and sometimes to each plantation.
- *Clearly defined objectives and methods*: collective demands were defined by each village assembly, then at the level of each plantation, each country and finally at the international scale; very quickly, collective actions became pivotal to the strategy and methods implemented by the organisations, including at a very local level.
- *Collective rules*: as leaders became empowered and the organisations became structured, collective and democratic ways of working were defined, which sustained the elected leaders' representativeness, accountability and collectively supported decision making. The tasks and responsibilities were shared out and roles defined. Group facilitation tools

taken from popular education methods helped to facilitate the members' participation and emancipation.

- *Resources*: each member paid dues to ensure the organisation's autonomy and means of action.

This community-organising model is also based on an incremental strategy that first targets small victories to strengthen the members' involvement and vision. Some local organisations were thus able to identify initial achievable victories (have an out-of-order borehole repaired by the company, develop a market place, or maintain the village's access routes), which helped to keep the residents involved over time, without discouragement, while at the same time seeking to gradually obtain more rights.

Concrete progress that shows it is possible

Increasing efforts enabled the local communities to win substantial victories. These included compensation totalling US$54,800 to 133 peasant families for crops destroyed by the LAC, the construction and repair of boreholes in some ten villages, the delivery of drinking water cisterns when the river used by Lendi village was polluted, the setting-up of a health centre, the extension of the power line in Mbambou and Dikola in Cameroon, recognition of the 142 hectares of sacred forest and community land in Cambodia along with a financial contribution for the ceremonies to appease the spirits, the integration of village children into plantation schools and the launch of the construction of a new school in Liberia.

These and other victories showed that the balance of power was gradually changing. In addition to the admittedly fragile dialogues set up, the media coverage of land grabbing by the Socfin and Bolloré Groups was an important victory for the local communities mobilised. Certainly, although the situation was still little known to the general public until a few years ago, the press articles, media reports and interviews have multiplied since 2015, which has gradually given visibility to the land conflicts and the multinational's abuses. In 2015, the World Bank's International Financial Corporation cancelled a loan under study for the Socfin Group apparently due to the existing and now visible conflicts. In December 2016, Socfin made a series of unilateral commitments under its CSR policy and, in early 2017, produced an action plan with a road map and complaints management process. To help set up its action plan, the Group hired The Forest Trust organisation (now EarthWorm). The verdicts of the libel lawsuits brought against the journalists and NGOs that published material on the subject reinforced the legitimacy of the struggle, and the Bolloré Group was even condemned several times in early 2019 for malicious prosecutions.

While Socfin's commitments are highly inadequate and the unilateral process unsatisfactory, the Transnational Alliance of Local Communities Affected by Socfin Bolloré Plantations has managed to gradually shift what once appeared to be immovable fronts, with support from a coalition of NGOs (Fian Belgium, Bread for All, Confédération Paysanne – Via Campesina France, GRAIN, ReAct, aGter, World Rainforest Movement, SOS Faim, Sherpa, and others). The building of a coalition of allies is another tool to strengthen the campaigns and makes it possible to pool a variety of skills and expertise in the form of surveys, media contacts, legal knowledge, capacity building and so on. The challenges of rebalancing power relations among the different actors in the value chains were huge. Strengths and skills have to be combined. As a Cameroonian proverb says, 'a single hand cannot fasten a bundle of wood'.

Increasing leverage to exert pressure

To reinforce the Transnational Alliance of villages defending their rights, the coalition of allies is now trying to activate different levers: media-related, legal and economic levers, particularly in Europe where the Socfin and Bolloré Groups are headquartered. Some of the avenues to be followed or further explored in order to rebalance the power relations among the different actors in this production chain and ensure a fairer value distribution throughout the chain include informing and calling for action from customers of the plantations' output, such as Michelin for rubber or Nestlé for palm oil, and from financiers like the ING bank. ReAct is keeping watch on the implementation the 2017 French law on the duty of care of parent companies and subcontractors, and investigating the financial arrangements and the Group's governance.

Conclusion

This experience thus gives hope that change is possible and will lead to an economy enabling workers, farmers and local communities to access the social, economic and environmental resources required for a decent standard of living. Although the progress made is minimal when compared to the violation of rights and environmental degradation experienced by these communities, this ongoing process can continue on its path and be further developed. Moreover, these experiences and the mistakes that may have been made have allowed a replicable model to be defined more precisely. One of the key lessons learnt is the importance of having robust, well-structured and democratic collective organisations. If campaigns are to succeed on a global scale, the local level must be extremely robust – effective coordination is impossible without well-structured local forces. The 'community-organising' tools developed within the different models bring a rigorous methodology to take this dimension further.

As a result of this experience, it seems crucial to develop the organisers' network worldwide in order to give professional support to mobilising citizens and workers so that value of production chains can be more fairly distributed. Experiences of citizens' associations capable of taking action on a wide range of issues have grown in number and strengthened this model, while greater resources will bring about the scale change needed to shift the global economy towards one based on the principles of solidarity and justice in the struggle against the impunity of multinationals.

Notes

1. www.socfin.com/sites/default/files/2020-04/2019%2012%2031%20 Organigramme%20Socfin_0.pdf
2. www.socfin.com/en/investors/socfin
3. Registration Document 2018, Bolloré, www.bollore.com/bollo-content/ uploads/2019/05/bollore_ddr_2018_gb_mel.pdf
4. 2018 Sustainability Report, Socfin, www.socfin.com/dashboard/download/ socfin-sustainability-report-2018/
5. 2018 Sustainability Report, Socfin, www.socfin.com/dashboard/download/ socfin-sustainability-report-2018/

References

Alinsky, S. (1969) *Reveille for Radicals*, 2nd edition, Vintage Books.

Alinsky, S. (1971) *Rules for Radicals: A Pragmatic Primer for Realistic Radicals*, Random House.

Gamson, W., Fireman, B. and Rytina, S. (1982) *Encounters With Unjust Authorities*, Dorsey.

Gurr, T. (1970) *Why Men Rebel*, Princeton University Press.

Oberschall, A. (1973) *Social Conflict and Social Movements*, Prentice-Hall.

Pouget, E. (2008 [1904]) *L'action directe*, Le Flibustier.

Sharp, G. (1973) *The Politics of Nonviolent Action*, Porter Sargent.

Conclusion: Pondering the future of global value chains

Florence Palpacuer and Alistair Smith

As the final touches are being put to this book, entire populations are submitted to compulsory confinement and curfew, a situation not experienced in many countries since the Second World War. The centralisation of governmental decisions is reaching new thresholds, together with the rarefaction of public spaces where pluralist views may be formed and expressed on our social, economic and political futures. Are we entering the 'new normal' of a digital age fed by GVCs and enforced through state repression? How can value chains be reshaped by social and political forces for a more sustainable 'world after'?

The research and activist perspectives collected in this book date from the 'world before', but they contain signals and analytical insights which can usefully inform such questions. Indeed, the rise of state authoritarianism and the mechanics of inequalities that GVCs have engendered or continue to build upon are becoming increasingly visible, while sustainability discourses are increasingly captured by lead players. While the citadels of political, financial and economic power which govern the GVCs may seem impregnable, a mosaic of bottom-up initiatives are stirring empowerment and emancipation, holding potential to reshape the social, economic and political forms of value chains.

Much has been said on the disruptions that the COVID-19 crisis would induce in our ways of operating in – and thinking about – the world economy. Some argue that the crisis is leading to greater awareness of the unsustainability of global growth, and that there is now an urgent need to revitalise local economies so as to meet the basic needs of their population in more reliable ways. A preceding wave of ideas had predicted massive changes based on the potential offered by so-called 4.0 ('fourth generation') technologies to provoke a relocation of manufacturing to the Global North. The two perspectives have at times been combined in ongoing speculation about the future of GVCs (see for instance, Fortunato, 2020).

As pointed out by several observers, however, to 'relocalise' – or 'reterritorialise' – value chains would involve sacrificing some substantial benefits derived from global scale economies and efficiencies (Miroudot, 2020), with unavoidable impacts on the capacity of dominant players to maintain above average returns on invested capital and, as such, to deliver the shareholder value that sustains their tight relationship to financial markets (Froud et al, 2006).

What is at stake therefore is nothing less than the core features of the business model developed by global lead firms and their large transnational suppliers, not to mention the intricate interdependencies that GVCs have established across countries, as analysed for instance by Gereffi (2020) in the case of medical supplies (also see Pananond et al, 2020).

GVCs have built up economic power of unprecedented reach on a global scale, operating through complex and diffuse layers of intermediaries that make both voluntary transformation and political regulation extremely difficult, all the more so when political powers are themselves tightly linked to the global hegemony, as emphasised by Martin Hess in the first chapter of this volume. To acknowledge the rise of state violence and authoritarianism in contemporary capitalism runs against some of our deepest premises in thinking about the global market economy, where democracy and emancipation have long been seen as concomitant with the economic opening of a growing number of countries throughout the world. Yet in the age of GVCs, as the social and ecological tensions that such an economic model generates continue to build up, coercion is increasingly used as a last-resort mechanism to ensure operational continuity, and calls for a re-assessment of the state's role in shaping society and the economy.

The multiplicity of ways in which the financial sphere is imbricated into these global productive formations and extracts the wealth they generate is only beginning to be uncovered, as Liam Campling and Clair Quentin do in their chapter on Global inequality chains. The speed, complexity, and opacity afforded by legal and technological advances in financial transactions have generated immaterial networks at a transnational scale, captured in the concept of the global wealth chain (Seabrooke and Wigan, 2014, 2017). These transactions have remained largely off the radars of GVC analysis despite the fact that these networks are an integral part of the value capture organised throughout global production systems. Hence, by making these patterns visible and understandable, the work of Campling and Quentin calls for reassessing the very nature of productive activities, the type of 'value' that workers generate through their contribution to GVCs, and how such value should be acknowledged, allocated and redistributed.

The dynamic nature of GVCs and the various ways in which they may be shaped and regulated in favour of greater sustainability are highlighted by Stefano Ponte, echoing the reflections of Martin Hess on the diversity of state roles in GVCs. The intricacies of economic and political forms of power in GVC formations, together with their state of continuous evolution, often lead to unexpected outcomes in the self-sustaining dynamics of global production, whereby sustainability initiatives are being 'reabsorbed' to fuel economic growth in ways that remain favourable to established powers. In the light of such characteristics, Ponte calls for new modes of 'orchestrating' GVCs that require a fine-tuned assessment of their power dynamics and a combination of diverse modes of regulatory intervention.

Taken together, and seen from a Gramscian perspective already deployed by Martin Hess in his chapter – albeit to discuss Gramsci's (1980) notion of the 'integral state' – these three chapters shed light on the 'historical bloc' formed of economic, political and ideological powers by which the hegemony of GVCs has been established and is being sustained, hence underscoring the challenges involved in developing counter-hegemonic initiatives that aim to reshape the forms of organisation of the global economy and their social/environmental outcomes.

A Gramscian prism also serves to highlight the unstable and incomplete nature of the hegemony, however, which always leaves spaces open for alternative approaches to form and grow, in an evolving struggle between competing ways of organising, regulating and thinking about the economy. Levy and Egan (2003) have acknowledged elsewhere the 'cascading effect' by which counter-hegemonic forces may induce broader social and political transformation: 'small perturbations can often be absorbed and accommodated with little impact on the overall structure. Periods of relative stability, however, are punctuated by discontinuity and change, as fissures split open and cascading reactions lead to major system-wide reconfiguration' (2003: 811).

In their contribution to this volume, Louise Curran and Jappe Eckhardt take stock of such moving, unstable features in the regulation of international trade to highlight a number of political opportunities that civil society groups might seize at the European level of trade policy, as the dominant economic rationale is being increasingly curbed by the need to consider social and political issues related to sustainability. Their informed discussion of the political opportunities offered by bilateral FTAs demonstrates the prominent role of civil society in shaping the normative foundations of the state regulatory apparatus, and the ongoing struggle between established interests on the one hand and more marginalised interests which could tip the Gramscian 'relations of force' in favour of more sustainable arrangements on the other.

Such a demonstration is extended in the first practitioner-authored chapter by Marilyn Croser who tackles the question of governmental regulation from the perspective of the UK-based activist coalition CORE. The coalition was among the first GVC-based civil society movements to voice the need for binding governmental regulation in the face of the lack of transformative capacity of voluntary firm-led 'corporate social responsibility' initiatives. From the Companies Act 2006 to the Modern Slavery Act 2015 and more recent legislative initiatives in France, Switzerland and the UK, her chapter uncovers the longstanding battles by which civil society promotes new laws, sees its demands circumvented in governmental responses, and adjusts its collective strategies to progressively scale up the regulatory framework from the national to the European level, in defence of enabling rights for vulnerable or deprived stakeholders in GVCs.

Christophe Alliot's description of BASIC's approach to objectivising societal costs reveals another of the key transformative strategies to rebalance asymmetries of power and therefore of negotiating capability in global economic chains: the internalisation of 'externalised' social and environmental costs. A deeper understanding of real-world data – and the context and choices made by those who produce and publish these data – enables this cooperative think-tank to arm citizens and consumers with a powerful tool to articulate, and indeed accelerate, societal demands for better distribution of gains within GVCs. In turn, the dialogues and negotiations, both societal and commercial, that the approach is designed to encourage and support are posited as the means through which processes of redistributing value more equitably between the asymmetrically positioned economic stakeholders along chains can take place, be they either transnationalised tropical product GVCs (cocoa/chocolate or coffee) or more local/territorial and regional value chains (such as dairy products in France, or staple food crops within West Africa).

Beyond the discussions generated directly by this chapter lie other related processes towards societal cost internalisation that are gaining considerable momentum, such as the movement for living wages and incomes for those employed at the beginning of GVCs. Albeit primarily North-driven at its origin, this movement is gearing up and coordinating its advocacy strategies, targeting – and promoting engagement with – lead firms and large-scale intermediaries that produce profit margins sufficient to share back down supply chains with those actors in fields, factories, mines or call centres whose voices have not been heard until the past two or three decades.

The pricing strategies and the precise mechanisms for achieving a more equitable distribution of value along the chains, using the concept of societal cost internalisation, are still in the process of discussion and definition, but Alistair Smith's description of nearly three decades of work in the fresh banana industry sheds light on some of the ingredients that such industry-specific strategies require, arguably as a *sine qua non* for their success. Smith's chapter shows how, despite their historically weak voice and bargaining power, organised workers in industrial-scale plantations and packhouses in Central and South America and Africa, in alliance with organised small-scale family farmers from the Philippines to the Caribbean to South America, have used the leverage of the lead firms' biggest selling food line not only to secure a place at the table, but to help set the agenda discussed there.

Critically, such an agenda covers the whole range of 'sustainability' topics discussed in the permanent multi-stakeholder WBF: social, economic and environmental. Separating these dimensions of sustainability into distinct 'boxes', with parallel and at times disconnected processes of debate, advocacy and collaborative action, as can be observed in many multi-stakeholder processes, is not only intellectually problematic, but appears highly unlikely to lead to transformative results for workers and producers, even less so if these crucial wealth generators are unorganised, unaware of the dynamics and the players downstream in the rest of the chain to consumers, and unprepared for direct engagements with lead firms over alternative emancipatory strategies.

Such a 'bottom-up' organising approach is adopted and emphasised by the activist initiative ReAct in support of the communities affected by various GVC-linked agro-industrial operations in Africa. The chapter by Eloïse Maulet describes the prerequisites for community organising and illustrates the concrete unfolding of the empowerment strategies that this French-based civil society group has developed. Their work draws inspiration from various forms of community organising initially adopted and conceptualised in a Northern context by radicals such as Saul Alinsky in the US or Emile Pouget in France.

Although gains may often be modest, and slow to have been obtained – and sometimes at high cost – for the mobilised stakeholders in these counter-hegemonic struggles, the diverse approaches highlighted in this book are paving the way for more radical changes that the succession of social, financial and ecological crises already experienced and still foreseeable will most undoubtedly trigger in coming years.

While the capacity for voluntary self-transformation of GVCs' 'historical bloc' is inevitably hampered by the intricacies of vested interests and the unprecedented scale at which they have been deployed in the world economy, as most clearly demonstrated in the first part of this volume, the second part of the book highlighted several facets of the transformative potential of civil society which may prove to become increasingly pervasive throughout the political and economic spheres, in a future which may come quicker than we are trained to envision.

The book itself can actually be seen as an outcome of one such 'fissure' in the global neoliberal hegemony insofar as it mobilised academic and activist resources in an emancipatory initiative vis-à-vis the processes of 'corporatisation' at work in both academic and NGO spheres. To divert academic time from delivering financially-rewarded, standardised academic production that productivity constraints have rendered increasingly incompatible with the generation of genuine knowledge is indeed a form of academic resistance. The emerging criteria for 'university social responsibility' that seek to account for the societal usefulness and outreach of academic work are only weakly rewarded in an environment of continuous assessment and competitive pressures to which academic institutions are now being submitted (Slaughter and Leslie, 1997; Engwall, 2008; Butler et al, 2017).

Likewise, pressures to build up economies of scale, raise funding and deliver accountability are increasingly pushing the most prominent civil society organisations to mimic the GVC lead firms' management systems and rationales (Alexander and Weiner, 1998; Dauvergne and LeBaron, 2014), while concerns have been voiced regarding the North-driven agenda of GVC-based activism (Palpacuer, 2019). In a counter-current to such trends, examples are provided in this book of activist initiatives that sustain counter-hegemonic capacity through 'bottom-up' GVC-based strategies to empower workers and small producers by promoting enabling rights, emancipatory analytics, and organising and bargaining capacities in favour of these previously invisible yet prominent contributors to economic 'value' and activity.

In developing this publication, we followed the lead of earlier initiatives (Appelbaum and Robinson, 2005; Hale and Wills, 2005) to combine academic and activist voices in a hybrid space of engaged scholarship and theoretically-informed activism, so as to foster the rethinking and reshaping of value chains. Fifteen years after these seminal joint calls for GVC transformation, the need is ever more pressing to regain our capacity to shape the territorial, ecological and social embeddedness of value chains in truly sustainable ways. Through our contribution, we wish to stir momentum for a broader engagement of stakeholders in and around value chains towards such a transformative project.

References

Alexander, J. and Weiner, B. (1998) The adoption of the corporate governance model by non-profit organizations, *Nonprofit Management and Leadership*, 8(3): 223–42.

Appelbaum, R. and Robinson, W.I. (eds) (2005) *Critical Globalization Studies*, Routledge.

Butler, N., Delaney, H. and Slywa, M. (2017) The labour of academia, *Ephemera: Theory and Politics in Organization*, 17(3): 467–80, editorial, special issue.

Dauvergne, P. and LeBaron, G. (2014) Protest, Inc.: *The Corporatization of Activism*, Wiley.

Engwall, L. (2008) The university: a multinational corporation?, in L. Engwall and D. Weaire (eds) *The University in the Market*, Portland Press, pp 9–21.

Fortunato, G. (2020) How COVID-19 is changing global value chains, UNCTAD News, 2 September, https://unctad.org/news/how-covid-19-changing-global-value-chains

Froud, J., Johal, S., Leaver, A. and Williams, K. (2006) *Financialization and Strategy. Narrative and Numbers*, Routledge.

Gereffi, G. (2020) What does the COVID-19 pandemic teach us about global value chains? The case of medical supplies, *Journal of International Business Policy*, 3(3): 287–301.

Gramsci, A. (1980) *Selections from the Prison Notebooks*, edited and translated by Quintin Hoare and Geoffrey Nowell Smith, International Publishers.

Hale, A. and Wills, J. (eds) (2005) *Threads of Labour: Garment Industry Supply Chains from the Workers' Perspective*, Blackwell.

Levy, D. and Egan, D. (2003) A neo-Gramscian approach to corporate political strategy: Conflict and accommodation in the climate change negotiations, *Journal of Management Studies*, 40: 803–29.

Miroudot, S. (2020) Reshaping the policy debate on the implications of COVID-19 for global supply chains, *Journal of International Business Policy*, DOI:10.1057/s42214-020-00074-6.

Palpacuer, F. (2019) Contestation and activism in global value chains, in G. Gereffi, S. Ponte and G. Raj-Reichert (eds) *Handbook on Global Value Chains*, Edward Elgar Publishing, pp 199–213.

Pananond, P., Gereffi, G. and Pedersen, T. (2020) An integrative typology of global strategy and global value chains: the management and organization of cross-border activities, *Global Strategy Journal*, 10(3), DOI: 10.1002/gsj.1388.

Seabrooke, L. and Wigan, D. (2014) Global wealth chains in the international political economy, *Review of International Political Economy*, 21(1): 257–63.

Seabrooke, L. and Wigan, D. (2017) The governance of global wealth chains, *Review of International Political Economy*, 24(1): 1–29.

Slaughter, S. and Leslie, L. (1997) *Academic Capitalism: Politics, Policies, and the Entrepreneurial University*, The Johns Hopkins University Press.

Index

Note: Page numbers in *italic* refer to figures; those in **bold** refer to tables.

4.0 ('fourth generation')
    technologies 173
4C (Common Code for the Coffee
    Community) 68

A

ACORN (Association of
    Community Organizations
    for Reform Now) 166, 167
ACP (Africa Caribbean Pacific
    Group) 93n1
activism 6–7, 178–80
    see also BASIC (Bureau
        d'Analyse Sociétale pour
        une Information Citoyenne/
        Bureau of Societal Analysis
        for Citizens' Information),
        France; BL (Banana
        Link); CORE (Corporate
        Responsibility Coalition,
        now Corporate Justice
        Coalition); ReAct (Réseaux
        pour l'Action collective
        internationale), France
Adidas 109
Africa
    gender equality policies 147–8
Africa Caribbean Pacific Group
    (ACP) 93n1
AgroParisTech (French Agronomy
    School) 121
Albert Heijn 62

Aldi 109, 139–40
Alford, M. 21
Alinsky, Saul 166, 167, 178
Alliance for Corporate
    Transparency 106–7
Amazon UK/Luxembourg tax
    structuring 46
anger, and community
    activism 157–8, 158–60
Argentina 71
Asda/Walmart 140–1
Association of Community
    Organizations for Reform
    Now (ACORN) 166, 167
austerity policies 18
Austria 109
authoritarian neoliberalisms 8, 27
    see also neoliberalism

B

Bair, J. 4–5
Banafair 136
banana GVC
    BASIC's impact assessment
        of 115, 130
    BL (Banana Link), UK 11–12,
        133–4, **148**, 148–9, 177–8
    1998 to 2005 period 138–40
    background and context 135–8
    challenging retailers 140–1
    gender equality 146–8
    ground up proposals 145–6

lead firms 134, **135**, 139–40,
143–5, 146, 147, **148**, 148–9
WBF (World Banana
Forum) 141–3, 145, 146,
149, 178
EU (European Union) 82, 84
Bangladesh
garment GVC 52
workers' rights 91–2
bargaining power 59
biofuels GVC 71–2
coffee GVC 61–2
BASIC (Bureau d'Analyse
Sociétale pour une
Information Citoyenne/
Bureau of Societal Analysis
for Citizens' Information),
France 10–11, 114–15,
130–1, 176–7
background and context 115–18
beyond value distribution 128–30,
129
information gaps in
GVCs 118–20
quantitative and qualitative
methods combined 120–2,
123, 124, *125–6*
value chain systemic
model 126–8
BATNAs (Best Alternative To
Negotiated Agreement) 163
beef GVC, BASIC's impact
assessment of 115
Belgium 15
biofuel GVC 9, 56, **66–7**, **69–70**,
71–2, *73*, 74–7
BL (Banana Link) 11–12, 133–4,
148, 148–9, 177–8
1998 to 2005 period 138–40
background and context 135–8
challenging retailers 140–1
gender equality 146–8
ground up proposals 145–6
lead firms 134, **135**, 139–40,
143–5, 146, 147, **148**, 148–9
WBF (World Banana Forum)
formation 141–3, 178
Bolloré group 12, 152, 153, 158,
160–1, 164–5, 168, 169, 170

Brazil
biofuel GVC 71, 74
coffee GVC 64
Mercosur-EU FTA 86–7
Brexit 18, 19, 33
Bribery Act 2010, UK 110
British Retail Consortium 105
Bruff, I. 27

C

Cambodia 12
garment GVC 27, 30, 52
land dispossession 26–7
palm oil and rubber
plantations 153, 154, 155,
157, 162, 164, 166, 168
state coercion 30
workers' rights 91
Cameroon
cocoa GVC 128
palm oil and rubber
plantations 153, 154–5, 156,
157, 159, 160, 161, 162,
164–5, 166, 167, 168
'cascading effect' 175
Central America 146–7
'chain governance' 39
Chief Trade Enforcement Officer
(CTEO), EU 89
China
cotton GVC 52
state influence on businesses 22
trade disputes with US 18,
19, 24
working conditions 41
Chiquita 134, 139, 146
Christian Aid 140
civil society organisations 2, 5–7,
25, 26
see also BASIC (Bureau
d'Analyse Sociétale pour
une Information Citoyenne/
Bureau of Societal Analysis
for Citizens' Information),
France; BL (Banana
Link); CORE (Corporate
Responsibility Coalition,
now Corporate Justice
Coalition); ReAct (Réseaux

pour l'Action collective internationale), France

climate change 115
see also environmental issues

cocoa GVC, BASIC's impact assessment of 10, 115, 118, 126–30, *129*, 130, 175–6

coffee GVC 9, 10, 56, 61–2, *63*, 64–5, **66–7**, 68, **69–70**, 71
BASIC's impact assessment of 118, 119–20, 121–2, *123*, 124, *125–6*, 130, 131, 175–6

collective action
theories of 160
see also ReAct (Réseaux pour l'Action collective internationale), France

Collombat, Benoit 160

Colombia
banana GVC 136
coffee GVC 124, *126*
violence against workers 28

COLSIBA (Latin American Banana Workers' Union Coordinating Body) 136, 137, 138, 146, 147

combinatory efforts 76, 77
coffee GVC 68

Common Code for the Coffee Community (4C) 68

Companies Act 2006, UK 103–4, 106, 107, 176

company law
company reports 107–8
UK review of 102–4

conflict resolution, four-step staircase tool 158, *159*

Conservation International 65

constitutive power 59, 60, 77
biofuels GVC 75–7
coffee GVC 64–5

Coop 139

CORE (Corporate Responsibility Coalition, now Corporate Justice Coalition) 10, 100–4, 112
background and context 99–100
mandatory HRDD and parent company liability 108–11

and the Modern Slavery Act 2015 104–6
monitoring and enforcement issues 106–8

corporate legal accountability *see* CORE (Corporate Responsibility Coalition, now Corporate Justice Coalition)

Corporate Responsibility Bill, UK 102–3

Corporate Responsibility Coalition, now Corporate Justice Coalition (CORE) *see* CORE (Corporate Responsibility Coalition, now Corporate Justice Coalition)

corporate social responsibility (CSR) *see* CSR (corporate social responsibility)

Cosmetic Warriors Ltd & Anor v Amazon.co.uk Ltd and Anor [2014] EWHC 181 [Ch]. 46

Costa Rica 91
banana GVC 136, 140–1

Côte d'Ivoire
cocoa GVC 128
palm oil and rubber plantations 153, 154, 161, 162, 164, 165, 166

COVID-19 pandemic 1, 3, 18, 22, 32–3, 116, 144, 173

cross-border financial flows 43

CSR (corporate social responsibility) 25, 65
see also CORE (Corporate Responsibility Coalition, now Corporate Justice Coalition)

CTEO (Chief Trade Enforcement Officer), EU 89

D

dairy GVC, BASIC's impact assessment of 115

Dallas, M.P. 59–60

Davies, Jonathan 25–6

deforestation 111, 119, 155

de-globalisation 32

deindustrialisation 4

Del Monte 134, 139

demonstrative power 59–60, 77
  biofuels GVC 72, 74
  coffee GVC 62, 64
Department for International
  Development, UK 140
'*Devoir de Vigilance*' (Duty of
  Vigilance) law, France 10,
  100, 109, 110, 111
direct action 163–4
directive orchestration 57, 60, 77
Dole 134, 139
Dominica 135
Drug GSP, EU 82, 93
Duty of Vigilance ('*Devoir de
  Vigilance*') law, France 10,
  100, 109, 110, 111

E

Earthworm (Forest Trust) 169
EBA (Everything But Arms) 91
economic nationalism 32–3
Ecuador 128
Egan, D. 175
Egypt 28
Engels, Friedrich 24
environmental issues 1–2, 5, 7
  state policy instruments 8–9
  see also BASIC (Bureau
    d'Analyse Sociétale pour
    une Information Citoyenne/
    Bureau of Societal Analysis
    for Citizens' Information),
    France; CORE (Corporate
    Responsibility Coalition,
    now Corporate Justice
    Coalition); ReAct
    (Réseaux pour l'Action
    collective internationale),
    France; sustainability
Ethiopia
  coffee GVC 119, 121, 124, *125*
ETI (Ethical Trading
  Initiative) 101, 105, 140
  Base Code on Labour
    Standards 141
EU (European Union)
  biofuels GVC 71, 74–5
  corporate due diligence 109, 112

NFRD (Non-Financial
  Reporting Directive) 10,
  100, 104, 106, 108–9
RED (Renewable Energy
  Directive [2009/28/EC])
  74–5, 76
trade policy 80–1, 175–6
  banana GVC 136, 138
  context 82–5
  FTAs (Free Trade
    Agreements) 9, 85–9, 176
  GSP (Generalized System of
    Preferences), 82, 84, 85,
    90–2, 93
  TSD (trade and
    sustainable development)
    chapters 85, 87–8
EUROBAN (European Banana
  Action Network) 84, 136–7
EuropeAid 118, 126
European Agriculture
  Commissioner 84
European Banana Action Network
  (EUROBAN) 84, 136–7
European Union (EU) *see* EU
  (European Union)
Export Processing Zones 21

F

Facebook 49
facilitative orchestration 57, 60, 77
Fairtrade certification 6
  banana GVC 137, 145
  coffee GVC 62
FAO 118, 126, 130
  Inter-Governmental Group
    on Bananas and Tropical
    Fruit 142
Farmers' Link 136, 137
financial flows 7, 8
Financial Reporting Council
  (FRC) 107–8
financial upgrading, in GVCs 44,
  46, *54*
financialisation 5, 44, 46, 52
Finland 109
'flexibilisation' of labour 31
Forest Trust (Earthworm) 169

four-step staircase tool for conflict resolution 158, *159*
France 15
  '*Devoir de Vigilance*' (Duty of Vigilance) law 10, 100, 109, 110, 111
FRC (Financial Reporting Council) 107–8
Free Ports 21
free trade 21
Free Trade Agreements (FTAs), EU 9, 85–9, 176
French Revolution 1789 160
Fresh Del Monte 141
fruits GVC, BASIC's impact assessment of 115
FTAs (Free Trade Agreements), EU 9, 85–9, 93
Fyffes 134, 139

G

GAF (Globalization Adjustment Fund), EU 89
'gamification' 28
garment GVC 4, 27, 30, 52
Gebana 136
Geest 136
gender issues 7
  banana GVC 146–8
  palm oil and rubber plantations 155
Generalized System of Preferences (GSP), EU 82, 84, 85, 90–2, 93
Gereffi, Gary 2
Germany 109
Ghana 128
GICs (global inequality chains) 8, 36–8, *47*, 49–51, 174
gig economy 28
Glassman, J. 22, 23
global financial crisis, 2008 3, 4, 18, 32, 33
global inequality chains (GICs) 8, 36–8, *47*, 49–51, 174
global production networks (GPNs) *see* GPNs (global production networks)

Global Resource Initiative Taskforce 111
global value chains (GVCs) *see* GVCs (global value chains)
global wealth chains (GWCs) 8, 28, 37–8, 38–41, *39*, 43–4, 46, *47*, 48–9, 51, *54*, 174
Globalization Adjustment Fund (GAF), EU 89
GM crops 72
Google 49
GPNs (global production networks) 17–19, 31–3
  and the integral state 19, 24–8, **26**, 32
    labour control 19, 27–31, *29*, *30*, 32
  state roles in 19, 20–4, **21**, 32
Gramsci, Antonio 12, 19, 25–6, 27, 175, 176
  see also integral state
grassroots action *see* BL (Banana Link); ReAct (Réseaux pour l'Action collective internationale), France
Great Depression, 1920s–1930s 33
Grenada 135
GSP (Generalized System of Preferences), EU 9, 82, 84, 85, 90–2, 93
Guatemala 136
GVCs (global value chains) 1–2
  controversies and critiques of 4–6
  definition of 36–7
  future of 172–80
  global hegemony of 174
  governance and power in 58–60, 174–5
  information on impact of (*see* BASIC (Bureau d'Analyse Sociétale pour une Information Citoyenne/ Bureau of Societal Analysis for Citizens' Information), France)
  overview of 2–3, *3*
  state role in 8–9, 59, 174
  and value capture 38–41, *39*, 48, 51, 52

GWCs (global wealth chains) 8, 28, 37–8, 38–41, *39*, 43–4, 46, *47*, 48–9, 51, *54*, 174

H

hegemony 12, 25, 174, 175
Honduras 28
Horner, R. 20–1, **21**, 22, 23
HRDD (human rights due diligence) 99–100, 106–7, 109, 111, 144
Huawei 22
human rights
  see also BASIC (Bureau d'Analyse Sociétale pour une Information Citoyenne/ Bureau of Societal Analysis for Citizens' Information), France; CORE (Corporate Responsibility Coalition, now Corporate Justice Coalition); ReAct (Réseaux pour l'Action collective internationale), France
Human Rights Council 99
human rights due diligence (HRDD) 99–100, 106–7, 109, 111, 144
human trafficking 104, 105, 106
Hymer, S. 50

I

ICA (International Coffee Agreement) 61, 64, 68
ILO (International Labour Organization) 17, 86, 90, 93
IMF (International Monetary Fund) 17
impact of GVCs *see* BASIC (Bureau d'Analyse Sociétale pour une Information Citoyenne/Bureau of Societal Analysis for Citizens' Information), France
India
  cotton GVC 52
  EU FTA 93

Indonesia
  biofuels GVC 71
  garment GVC 52
'industrial upgrading' 5
inequality *see* GICs (global inequality chains)
information, on impact of GVCs *see* BASIC (Bureau d'Analyse Sociétale pour une Information Citoyenne/ Bureau of Societal Analysis for Citizens' Information), France
ING Bank 170
injustice, and community activism 158–60
INSEE 118
institutional power 59, 60, 77
  biofuels GVC 74–5
  coffee GVC 64
intangible assets 43, 48
integral state 19, 24–8, **26**, 32, 175
  and labour control 19, 27–31, *29*, *30*, 32
intellectual property 42–3, 52
interest alignment 57, 58
  biofuels GVC 77
  coffee GVC 68, 71
Inter-Governmental Group on Bananas and Tropical Fruit, FAO 142
International Banana Conferences 138–9, 141–2
International Coffee Agreement (ICA) 61, 64, 68
International Labour Organization (ILO) 17, 86, 90, 93
International Monetary Fund (IMF) 17
International Trade Union Confederation (ITUC) 28, *29*, 30, *30*, 31
International Union of Agriculture and Foodworkers (IUF) 138
ISCC (International Sustainability and Carbon Certification) 74–5
issue visibility 57–8, 77
  biofuels GVC 76–7
  coffee GVC 68, 71

Italy 139
ITUC (International Trade Union
    Confederation) 28, *29*, 30,
    30, 31
IUF (International Union
    of Agriculture and
    Foodworkers) 138

J

J. Sainsbury 139
Japan 86, 87
Jessop, Bob 23
Joint Committee on
    Human Rights, UK
    Parliament 110–11

K

Kraft 62

L

labour control
    and GICs (global inequality
        chains) 49–50
    and the integral state 19, 27–31,
        29, *30*, 32
labour-power 40–1
LAC (Liberian Agricultural
    Company) 157, 162–3,
    166, 168
land rights and dispossession 26–7
    see also ReAct (Réseaux
        pour l'Action collective
        internationale), France
Latin America 41
Latin American Banana Workers'
    Union Coordinating Body
    (COLSIBA) 136, 137, 138,
    146, 147
lead firms 7, 173
    banana GVC 134, **135**, 139,
        143–5, **148**, 148–9
    GVC governance and
        power 58–9
    power of 31–2
    and value capture 39–40
legislation *see* CORE (Corporate
    Responsibility Coalition, now
    Corporate Justice Coalition)

Levy, D. 175
Liberia
    palm oil and rubber
        plantations 154, 155, 157,
        161, 162–3, 164, 166, 167
Liberian Agricultural Company
    (LAC) 157, 162–3, 166, 168
Lister, J. 57–8
local economies, revival of 173
Luxembourg 15
    Amazon UK tax structuring 46

M

MALOA (Malen Affected Land
    Owners and Land Users
    Association) 162
Marxian value theory 48
May, Theresa 105
Mayer, F. 43
Mercosur-EU FTA 86–7, 92
metagovernance 23
Meyer, T. 89
Michelin 170
Migros 139
Milberg, W. 43
mining products GVC, BASIC's
    impact assessment of 115
Modern Slavery Act, UK 10, 100,
    104–6, 108, 110, 176
money laundering 44
MSIs (multi-stakeholder
    initiatives) 25, 56
multinational corporations
    legal accountability (*see* CORE
        (Corporate Responsibility
        Coalition, now Corporate
        Justice Coalition))
    and taxation 43–4

N

National Audit Office, UK 108
nationalism 18
neo-Gramscian approaches 23–4
neoliberalism 18, 19, 25, 27
neo-Marxian approaches 23–4
neo-Ricardian approaches 48
neo-Weberian approaches 22, 23,
    24, 25

Nespresso 119, 121
Nestlé 109, 170
NFRD (Non-Financial Reporting Directive), EU 10, 100, 104, 106, 108–9
non-tariff barriers 21
non-violent action 163–4
Norway 145

O

Oberschall, Anthony 160
offshore banking 43
oil palm plantations *see* ReAct (Réseaux pour l'Action collective internationale), France
orchestration 77–8, 175
  biofuels GVC 76–7
  coffee GVC 65, **66–7**, 68, 71
Oxfam 65, 144–5

P

palm oil plantations *see* ReAct (Réseaux pour l'Action collective internationale), France
Paris Climate Accord 9, 86
peasant revolts 160
Perham, Linda 103
Peru 119, 124, *125*
pharmaceutical industries 33
Philippines 28
platform economy 31
populism 18
'post-democracy' 28
Pouget, Emile 164, 178
power, in GVCs (global value chains) 59–60, 174–5
Procter and Gamble 62
'production networks' 5
Public Accounts Committee, UK Parliament 108
public orchestration 57, 59, 68, 77
publishing GVC, BASIC's impact assessment of 115

R

Rainforest Alliance 62, 65

ReAct (Réseaux pour l'Action collective internationale), France 12, 152–3, 170–1, 178
  background and context 153–5
  collective organisation and action 155–64, 165–9
  transnational alliances 164–5, 169–70
RED (Renewable Energy Directive [2009/28/EC]), EU 74–5, 76
'relocalisation' of value chains 173
Réseaux pour l'Action collective internationale (ReAct), France *see* ReAct (Réseaux pour l'Action collective internationale), France
Responsible Global Value Chain (RGVC) initiative 6, 7
retail companies
  banana GVC 134, **135**, 139–40, 143–5, 146, 147, **148**, 148–9
Rethinking Value Chains (RVC) collective 6–7
RGVC (Responsible Global Value Chain) initiative 6, 7
rice GVC, BASIC's impact assessment of 115
rubber plantations *see* ReAct (Réseaux pour l'Action collective internationale), France
Rudé, George 160
RVC (Rethinking Value Chains) collective 6–7

S

Saint Lucia 135
Saint Vincent and the Grenadines 135
Seabrooke, L. 38
'self-employment' 28, 31
Sharp, Gene 163
shrimps GVC, BASIC's impact assessment of 115
Sierra Leone
  palm oil and rubber plantations 154, 162, 164

slavery 41, 104, 105, 106, 107
'slowbalisation' 32
small farmer-led activism *see* BL
    (Banana Link), UK
smile curve 41–3, *42*, 48, 51
Smith, A. 23, 24
Socfin Group 12, 152, 153–4,
    156, 157–8, 160, 161, 164–5,
    168–9, 170
  Socapalm subsidiary 156, 157,
    163, 165
social inequalities 1–2, 4, 7, 177
  see also BASIC (Bureau
    d'Analyse Sociétale pour
    une Information Citoyenne/
    Bureau of Societal Analysis
    for Citizens' Information),
    France; CORE (Corporate
    Responsibility Coalition, now
    Corporate Justice Coalition)
'social movement repertoire' 163
South America
  gender equality policies 146–7,
    147–8
South Korea
  EU FTA 87, 88
  garment GVC 30
  state coercion 30–1
South–South–North activism 11,
    137, 138, 139, 141–2, 144
Special Economic Zones 21
Starbucks 62
state
  role in GVCs 8–9, 59, 174
  roles in GPNs (global production
    networks) 19, 20–4, **21**, 32
    integral state 19, 24–8, **26**, 32
    labour control 19, 27–31, *29*,
    30, 32
state authoritarianism 1–2, 7, 8,
    19, 172, 174
  and labour control 19, 27–31,
    29, *30*
state coercion 24, 26–8
  modalities of 25–6
state purchasing policies 23
state-owned companies 22–3
strikes, suppression of 28
'Supermarket Scorecard' 144–5

sustainability 1–2, 7, 56–7,
    77–8, 172–3
  biofuel GVC 9, 56, 66–7,
    69–70, 71–2, 73, 74–7
  coffee GVC 9, 10, 56, 61–2, *63*,
    64–5, **66–7**, 68, **69–70**, 71
  EU policies 9
  governance and power in
    GVCs 58–60
  orchestration for 57–8, 77–8
    biofuels GVC 76–7
    coffee GVC 65, **66–7**, 68, 71
  see also environmental issues
Switzerland 10, 15, 109, 139
Synaparcam 162

T

tariffs 21
tax havens 43, 46, 48
tax systems 50–1, 52
  and GICs (global inequality
    chains) 50
  tax avoidance and evasion 43–4
tea GVC, BASIC's impact
    assessment of 115
temporary contracts 28
Tesco 139, 140–1, 147
textiles GVC
  BASIC's impact assessment
    of 115
  see also garment GVC
Tilly, Charles 163
TISA (Transparency in
    Supply Chains Act),
    California 104, 105
TISC (Transparency in Supply
    Chains) clause 104–6,
    107, 108–9
trade policy
  EU (European Union) 9, 80–1,
    175–6
    banana GVC 136, 138
    context 82–5
    FTAs (Free Trade
      Agreements) 9, 85–9, 176
    GSP (Generalized System of
      Preferences), 82, 84, 85,
      90–2, 93

TSD (trade and sustainable development) chapters 85, 87–8
transmission mechanism of power 59
Transnational Alliance of Local Communities Affected by Socfin/Bolloré Plantations 165, 166, 169–70
Transparency in Supply Chains (TISC) clause 104–6, 107, 108–9
Transparency in Supply Chains Act (TISA), California 104, 105
Trump, Donald 18, 33

U

Uber 31, 49
UK
  Companies Act 2006 103–4, 106, 107, 176
  company law review 102–4
  Modern Slavery Act 10, 100, 104–6, 108, 110, 176
UN Guiding Principles on Business and Human Rights 99
Unilever 109
'university social responsibility' 179
upgrading, in GVCs 40, 50–1, 51–2
  and the 'smile curve' 41–3, 42, 48, 51
US
  AGOA programme 82–3
  biofuels GVC 71, 74
  trade disputes with China 18, 19, 24

V

'value added' 37, 41–2, 49, 51
value capture 48, 115
value chains 5

'relocalisation' of 173
vegetables GVC, BASIC's impact assessment of 115
Vietnam 87, 92

W

Walmart 139, 140–1
WBF (World Banana Forum) 11–12, 145, 146, 149, 178
  formation of 141–3
Werner, M. 23
Wigan, D. 38
WINFA (Windward Islands Farmers' Association) 135, 137
women
  banana GVC 146–8
  palm oil and rubber plantations 155
  working conditions 41
workers' rights 27–8, 29, 30, 30
working conditions 41
  GVC-based activism 6, 7
  see also BASIC (Bureau d'Analyse Sociétale pour une Information Citoyenne/ Bureau of Societal Analysis for Citizens' Information), France; CORE (Corporate Responsibility Coalition, now Corporate Justice Coalition)
World Banana Forum (WBF) see WBF (World Banana Forum)
World Bank 17
  International Financial Corporation 169
world trade, overview of 2–3, 3
WTO (World Trade Organization) 3, 68, 82–5, 93, 138, 139

Z

Zara 131